PROMOTIONALS, 1934-1983

Dealership Vehicles in Miniature

by

Steve Butler

© 1997

Steve Butler

Published by

L-W BOOK SALES
PO Box 69
Gas City, Indiana 46933

<u>On the Cover</u>

- 1953 Ford F-100 pickup by Banthrico
- 1965 Plymouth Fury III by Jo-Han
- 1963 Chevrolet Impala SS by AMT
- 1967 Ford Mustang by AMT
- 1951-52 Nash Rambler by Banthrico
- 1969 Dodge Coronet R/T by MPC

———

———

The Author welcomes comments concerning the information in this book as well as promotionals that may be purchased to expand his collection. Please address these matters to:

Steve Butler
2696 Brookmar Dr.
York, PA 17404

Additional copies of this book may be ordered for $19.95 plus $3.00 for postage and handling from the Author at the above address or from the Publisher at:

L-W Book Sales
P.O. Box 69
Gas City, IN 46933

PROMOTIONALS, 1934-83
Dealership Vehicles in Miniature

TABLE OF CONTENTS

ACKNOWLEDGMENTS

Rosemary, my wife, provides understanding supplemented by considerable tolerance that encourages my toy related pursuits such as attending shows, collecting, writing and other endeavors. She is a willing and exemplary editor always improving my narratives. For these and numerous other reasons she deserves my admiration and gratitude. Clarence Young also deserves an acknowledgment. He was my associate in the AUTOQUOTES project for several years. Clarence is among the most knowledgeable and trustworthy persons in the toy hobby. Without these two individuals this book would be seriously lacking. Thanks also to the personnel at the Camera Center of York whose support of this fledgling photographer permitted photographic enhancement of this text.

PROLOG

Writing is not for me a profit-making venture. If it were, I'd try a novel. Rather, I write about things I like, which happen to be toy vehicles including promotionals. In the process and as a result, I meet new people and learn a few things.

Yesterday serves as a good example. An older friend named Walter has a son who owns several auto dealerships. Learning of this book writing effort, Walter suggested that I visit one of the dealerships and talk with a veteran salesman named Joe to discuss promotionals. Joe told me that in 1958 he won a new Cadillac. However, the car had not yet been delivered, so he received a promotional model of the car to look at while he waited. He sold the car immediately after its delivery but still has the promotional. At the end of the meeting Joe suggested that I head for another dealership to talk with Bob and Tom, both also seasoned veterans. It was Bob who related the story of the Chevrolet salesman who had a unique use for promotionals. The salesman made a deal with a local florist for a floral arrangement designed to include a promotional as the centerpiece. When the salesman sold a new car, he sent his customer as a thank you gesture the flower arrangement incorporating the promotional of the new car, in the proper color if possible.

So, in just one day I met three new acquaintances and learned some interesting facts such as the preceding promotional floral arrangement process. I hope that in your search for promotionals you find this book useful while making new friends and learning new things as I did just today.

Steve Butler

The Ford Motor Company introduced its revolutionary Mustang in 1964. It was given a 1964½ model year designation. To promote this first pony car, the company issued an attractive promotional version. Thousands were distributed through dealerships and mailed directly to potential customers. Most were either red or white.

The first Chrysler 300 was produced in 1955 and epitomized the balance of size, luxury and performance. By 1966, imitators such as Oldsmobile with its Starfire had appeared and disappeared. The Chrysler 300, as depicted by this promotional version, remained at the head of the class.

Willys introduced its Forward Control Jeep line in 1957. This cabover design was somewhat revolutionary in respect to light duty trucks of the era. For the introduction, the company also issued promotional versions of their FC-170 pickup and stake truck, an example of which is pictured.

Promotionals, the subject of this book, are miniature vehicles initially intended for use by car and truck dealerships and manufacturers to promote the sale of their products. Promotionals or promos, as they are called by most collectors, differ from toys in several ways. Promotionals are annual issues intended for distribution only during the model year of the vehicle they represent. They were no longer produced as dealer promotionals after that year. Vehicle manufacturers such as Buick and Chrysler contracted with the toy manufacturers for the production of promotionals. In contrast, toys were designed and produced at the discretion of toy manufacturers and were intended as children's playthings not for use as sales inducements. Most toys remained in toy manufacturers' product lines for multiple years. Some toys were adapted for promotional purposes, and most promotionals became toys as soon as they were acquired by children. This text generally encompasses only those miniature vehicles that were primarily designed for and issued under the auspices of vehicle manufacturers for promotional purposes.

Promotionals have a widespread appeal enjoyed by comparatively few collectibles. They are sought by diverse groups including:

Promotional collectors - Some collect based on an era; some collect only the products of one manufacturer such as Ford; some collect only plastic or metal versions; some try to collect them all.

Toy collectors - Promotionals look like toys and once in the hands of kids would soon become playthings. Promotionals thus meet the collecting criteria for many toy collectors and especially those who formerly played with them.

Automobilia collectors - Such collectors are interested in factory and dealership materials related to the automobile (including trucks) such as advertising brochures, jewelry, awards, marketing items and promotionals.

Advertising collectors - Dealership and financial institution information was frequently printed on promotionals for advertising purposes. Further, promotionals were often adapted by other businesses such as taxi companies, retail firms, trucking companies and even the U.S. Mail. They were also used for sporting events, beauty pageants and even world's fairs. Promotionals used for advertising purposes have unique markings and, sometimes, unique colors.

Model collectors - Promotionals, especially the plastic ones, are actually exact

This 1983 Camaro promotional is one of many in the $25 and under price range. These inexpensive vehicles are popular with beginning collectors both because of price and because they represent the first cars that many of the collectors and their peers owned or drove.

In the $100 to $200 price range there are a multitude of examples. This 1956 Desoto is one, and it offers several pluses. It is an orphan car, a make no longer produced. It has vintage, condition and an attractive two-tone paint scheme.

For the more than $500 buyer, this 1967 Camaro Indianapolis 500 pace car is a possibility. Early Camaro promotionals are desirable, and the Indy 500 decals add to its desirability. Note that the decals on this vehicle tolerate only minimal handling which has resulted in an inordinately few examples in optimum condition.

scale models made from the blueprints of full-sized vehicles. Consequently, they are of interest to many model collectors.

In addition to being of interest to multiple collector groups, promotionals are available for every pocketbook and can be collected by individuals of varying financial means. Examples are available in the $25 and under price range. Many are found in the $100 to $200 price bracket, and still others are valued at $500 or more for the advanced collector with a larger budget.

Promotionals appeal to persons of varied generations just as they do to individuals with varied budgets. Collectors tend to focus on the era of their youth and on the cars and trucks they have owned or always wanted. Thus, baby boomers tend to start with promotionals from the 1960's, collectors of their parents' ages tend to favor examples from the 1940's and into the 1950's, and the respective grandparents/parents prefer the 1930's vehicles. Typically, as their collections begin to fill with the promotionals of primary interest, collectors move forward or backward in time expanding their collections.

Unlike many fields of collecting, promotionals can be found in every area of the country. The original sources were primarily new car and truck dealerships, and those dealerships were scattered throughout the U.S. In addition to this diversity of original sources, examples can be found in the secondary market wherever collectibles turn up. Sources include toy shows, car shows and swap meets, antique shows and malls, auctions, flea markets, yard sales and more.

Promotional adaptations regularly found their way into retail stores, financial institutions, an assortment of businesses and other places. Typically, such promotionals differed from their counterparts in some manner. Those issued for sale in retail stores were generally of a generic color while most found at dealerships were actual colors of their full-sized counterparts. However, overruns of actual color production were sometimes distributed for retail store sales. Promotionals ordered by banks and savings and loans were of generic colors as well and had advertising imprints on their roofs. These examples were used as inducements for vehicle loans. Other companies and organizations ordered promotionals with special colors, advertising and, sometimes, features to represent their businesses. These vehicles were occasionally used as awards as well as for business promotions.

One final comment on the collectible appeal of promotionals: Several are of approximately 1/28th scale while the vast majority are closer to 1/25th scale. As such, promotionals are not overly large and display well on shelves and in display cases. They are appreciated as a collectible that does not require excessive space but still possesses that aura of nostalgia sought by collectors.

This 1934 Studebaker was distributed at the Chicago World's Fair in 1934. The casting for the trunk lid included the designation: "REPLICA OF GIANT WORLD'S FAIR STUDEBAKER"

This 1949 Dodge promotional is one of the first examples issued by National Products in 1/25th scale. Prior to 1949 most National Products promotionals were of smaller scale, about 1/28th or 1/30th. The company made a few smaller scale promotionals through 1950 (e.g., Buick and Nash) and continued others of smaller scale until the design of the actual vehicle changed (e.g., Dodge and Studebaker trucks).

Evolution of the Promotional

Toy vehicles were adapted for use as promotionals in the 1920's, perhaps earlier. As an example, in 1924 Chevrolet adapted cast iron toy renditions made by Arcade of Freeport, Illinois. Several 1930's models of Arcade Greyhound busses were issued with GMC markings and were also adapted for use as promotionals. By 1929, Tootsietoy (the trade name for Dowst Manufacturing Company of Chicago) had become a household name in the toy field. Ford used Tootsietoy's excellent miniature 1928 Model A coupe and sedan for promotional purposes. These toys were identical to those available in toy stores except that they were issued in small cardboard boxes matching the color of the car inside and marked only with "THE NEW *Ford.*" In 1935, Tootsietoy's LaSalles were similarly adapted for promotional use. Pressed steel 1933 Graham Silver Streak sedans measuring 19½ inches in length and made by Corcoran Manufacturing Company of Washington, Indiana were issued under the trade name Cor-Cor. These cars were adapted with slight modification as promotionals for Graham dealerships. During the mid-1930's several small rubber toys including Oldsmobiles, Pontiacs, Fords, Chryslers, Desotos and Studebakers were used as promotionals as well.

The World's Fair was held in Chicago in 1933 and continued into 1934. Studebaker decided to have a toy version of their 1934 President sedan made specifically for issue at the fair. They arranged for National Products of Chicago to produce the toy car for that purpose. "REPLICA OF GIANT WORLD'S FAIR STUDEBAKER" was cast in the trunk lid. This Studebaker at six inches long was of about 1/28th scale. It was made of an inexpensive metal alloy generally called pot metal or slush that was a popular material for smaller toys of the time. The miniature Studebaker rode on white rubber tires marked "Firestone" mounted on red wood hubs. Thus, Studebaker became the first automobile company to issue a promotional and National Products became the first maker.

The appeal of the small Studebaker was quickly recognized. Chrysler, Diamond T, Federal, Graham, Hudson, International and Reo were among the additional makes soon produced by National Products. Most would also be of approximately 1/28th scale except for a few, now very scarce items, that were much larger. By the late 1940's, AMT with their 1946 Ford and Master Caster with their Ford, Packard and Hudson of 1948 and 1949 vintages entered the promotional field. Their vehicles set the standard scale for subsequent promotionals at 1/25th. These two companies as well as National Products were soon overshadowed by Banthrico Industries of Chicago.

Banthrico Industries' origin was the Stronghart Company of Chicago which was formed in 1914. The company specialized in toy banks, especially ones for distribution to financial

The "K" on the hubcaps and above the grill might suggest that this toy is a promotional for the 1949-50 Kaiser Deluxe four-door convertible. The Kaiser logo and other matter on the original box confirm the car's promotional status. Interestingly, the grill of the car pictured on the box is that of a 1947-48 Kaiser. Most of these Kaisers are either maroon or aqua. The pictured car has an unusual color that would warrant a premium.   This is the only promotional made by Toy Founders.

The 1950-52 Nash Rambler is one of very few pot metal promotional convertibles. All were quite susceptible to breakage resulting in a minimal survival rate.

This Willys Jeep M-715 U.S. Army stake truck is the last dealer or factory promotional produced by Banthrico. Unlike its pot metal predecessors, it was not a bank and exhibits considerably more detail.

institutions. Around 1948 Banthrico acquired National Products and in 1949 issued their first promotionals marked "Banthrico." These 1949 models included Chrysler, Desoto, Dodge and Pontiac sedans plus a full line of body styles for Chevrolet and were marked "*by National Products* DIVISION BANTHRICO INDUSTRIES, INC.*" Within two years only Banthrico markings would appear on their 1/25th scale vehicles, all of which would be banks. The latter were accomplished by using a metal base plate with a coin slot within an access door on the undersides of the promotionals. Perhaps not coincidentally, Banthrico's products were adapted by financial institutions for promoting new vehicle loans about the same time. This new market increased the company's production volume and presumably reduced unit cost. Although the vehicle manufacturers (e.g., Ford, Chevrolet, etc.) probably lost some control of their promotional distribution in the process, they should have benefitted from reduced per unit manufacturing costs and improved exposure, the latter being the primary objective at the outset. The 1967 Willys Jeep M-715 is considered to be Banthrico's last pot metal promotional (excluding reissues). It was a factory promotional produced in conjunction with vehicles proposed for a U.S. Army contract.

By the time of Banthrico's entry into the promotional manufacturing field, many toy companies had achieved success with lines of toys made of plastic, a relatively new but promising material for such items. Plastic and its production process permitted increased accuracy and greater detail than allowed by pot metal. Further, painting problems could be avoided. These factors were quickly recognized by both vehicle manufacturers and would-be manufacturers of promotionals. Some companies such as Cruver (1949 Oldsmobile), Hudson (1949 Hudson), and Toy Founders (1949 Kaiser) would produce a single promotional and leave the market. Other companies who entered the field became dominant manufacturers of promotionals. These included AMT Corporation beginning with their renditions of Fords, Studebakers, Plymouths and Pontiacs and Product Miniature Company (PMC) with their versions of Chevrolets and Internationals. Banthrico made an early attempt using plastic with their 1951 Kaiser Henry J and remained a factor in the promotional market with varied pot metal renditions until 1956.

Exterior Developments

Throughout their production era and with very few exceptions, pot metal promotionals had single-piece body castings that included all details (e.g., bumpers, chrome trim, windows, etc.). The exceptions included the application of windshields and window frames for convertible models, and those were limited to 1949 and 1950 Chevrolets, the 1949 Packard and the 1950-52 Rambler. The unique construction of these few vehicles was very fragile making complete examples quite rare and correspondingly valuable today. The primary exterior variable for pot metal cars was their color(s). Chevrolet, Nash, Packard, Hudson and several Chrysler Corporation models were among the promotionals issued in the actual colors of their full-sized counterparts. Beautiful two-tone combinations, popular with the motoring public, were issued by the first four named companies as well.

These 1958 Pontiac Bonnevilles were made by AMT for retail store distribution. Note that the exterior trim and seat inserts are painted gold, changes typically found on retail store issues. Both cars have their original boxes and do not exhibit the warpage generally found on Pontiac promotionals of this vintage.

This 1954 Plymouth taxi has molded-in bumpers indicating that it was likely produced for retail store distribution as were the above Pontiacs. Taxi versions of promotionals command a premium because they appeal to persons who collect cab-related items.

A few years after Banthrico entered the pot metal promotional market, they became the dominant maker. At that time they began to produce vehicles mostly in generic colors. This practice reduced the differentiation by color between promotionals issued by vehicle makers and those issued by financial institutions. In fact, one end flap on some Banthrico boxes lists the possible colors of the cars with a space for a check mark. (All possible makes of vehicles were printed in the same manner. Pencil was used for content notations.) Those colors listed were:

Red	Light green
Dark blue	Maroon
Light Blue	Gold
Dark green	Cream

The shades varied from year to year, and gold and cream must have been minimally used.

Makers of plastic promotionals exhibited more variances in their exterior design features: These features included:

Types of plastic
Colors
Materials used for trim pieces
Use of windows
Interiors visible from the outside

Plastic came in several "flavors" all with difficult to pronounce and to remember names. For purposes of this book, plastic came in two types, warping and nonwarping. The primary distinction between the two types of plastic is found in their designations. Curiously, some manufacturers used both types of plastic while others were slow to make the change to the virtues of nonwarping plastic. Most of the earliest plastic promotionals through the 1950's and for some makers, until 1963, were made of warping plastic. When subjected to heat, warping plastic vehicles would begin to alter directions around their strongest points, resulting in designs unique to that year of issue and not intended by their makers. The warping tendency is somewhat reduced for such cars with painted surfaces. (See Notes on Reissues in Section 3.)

Plastic could be molded in just about any color including actual or factory colors used by the vehicle manufacturers ordering the promotionals. Those not molded in factory colors could easily be painted. Because promotionals could be used to depict colors as well as designs, the options offered by plastic better met market needs. In addition, promotional manufacturers could differentiate between factory/dealership and retail store examples using colors. The latter were generally made in generic colors and often had different interior and exterior trim colors, sometimes substituting gold and silver. (See Notes on Reissues in Section 3.)

Friction motors in plastic promotionals are quite common and often an indication that the vehicle is a retail store not a dealer car. Friction motors are very rare in pot metal promotionals appearing only in Master Caster vehicles such as the 1948-49 Hudson pictured above. Given their rarity, friction-powered pot metal promotionals warrant a premium value over corresponding coaster versions.

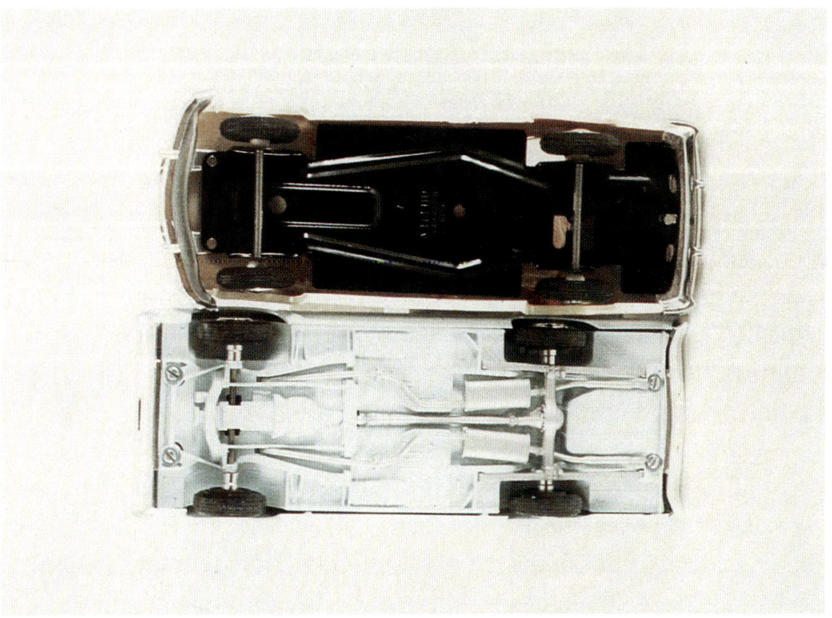

The metal chassis pictured above is on a 1951 Pontiac. Although the chassis has provision for a wind-up motor, none was installed. This is one indication that it was a dealer promotional. The plastic chassis below is on a 1965 Pontiac dealer promotional. It has the gray molded plastic underside features that add to the realism of some of the mid-1960's promotionals.

Trim pieces used for plastic promotionals could be included in the molds or applied. Bumpers were initially made of metal, later, plastic. Some of the least costly retail store renditions had molded-in as opposed to applied bumpers. Chrome trim such as hood and fender ornaments were usually separately applied items, especially on promotionals of later issue. One notable example was the 1949 Oldsmobile promotional made by Cruver. Virtually all of the exterior trim on that car was plated and applied including the door handles.

Windows were another manufacturing variable especially on the earliest issues. Polished metal, clear plastic and plastic painted silver on the inside were approaches used.   When realistic interiors began to appear in promotionals around 1956, the clear plastic option became the selected approach for windows.   However, for most of these and future factory promotionals, only clear front and rear windows would be used and the side windows remained open or blank. Promotional manufacturers frequently eliminated windows and deleted interiors for some of the lower cost versions for retail store sales.

Underside Changes

Changes in promotional designs could be observed from the undersides of the vehicles as well. These changes encompassed approaches from combinations of the following:

        Key-wind motors
        Friction motors
        Coaster models
        Bank slots
        Metal chassis/base plate
        Plastic chassis/base plate
        Mounting hardware

With rare exceptions, pot metal promotionals were coasters, vehicles with no motor mechanism for power. The exceptions include the very limited number of Hudson and Ford promotionals issued by Master Caster that are quite scarce and commensurately valuable today. The remainder of the pot metal coaster examples were issued with or without metal base plates. Vehicles with base plates made by Banthrico after about 1950 would have bank slots as well.

Plastic promotionals employed most of the possible underside combinations. Early models such as the 1949 Fords and the 1951 Studebakers had key-wind motors on a steel chassis. Some early models for dealership issue were coasters that used the same steel chassis without the key-wind motor. Later, the friction motor replaced the key-wind motor still using a steel chassis. The friction motor would then also be eliminated from some promotionals resulting in coasters for dealership issue. It should be noted here that some of the factory promotionals

The photo above shows a group of employees at Hudson putting the final touches on their 1948-49 plastic promotional. This car was issued in two-tone paint schemes with the paint applied on the inside of the clear plastic. Examples were also issued with bodies half painted and half clear. The lady in the left foreground seems to be polishing a stack of half- painted cars and the lady to the right has one to wrap and box. The adjacent photo is a finished product.

by AMT used aluminum not steel for the chassis on their coaster versions. Continuing with the motor/chassis possibilities, plastic then superseded steel as the primary chassis material. Most of the retail store issue promotional versions became friction-powered, plastic chassis vehicles. Dealership issue vehicles were primarily plastic chassis coaster models, but some were also issued with friction motors as well.

While some of the early plastic promotionals followed the motor/no motor path, others continued the dual use of promotionals as banks that was introduced by Banthrico for their pot metal renditions. A bank chassis was used for Chevrolet promotionals from 1949 through 1957. Plastic was used for these Chevrolets' chassis although the removable bank access plates changed from steel to plastic during that time frame. Note that some dealership issues of these Chevrolets (1957's for example) could have a bank, friction or coaster chassis.

The means used to attach the chassis to vehicle bodies also varied over time. Pins, one-way screws, rivets, screw-like nails, normal screws and even glue were used. Pot metal promotionals used pins, one-way screws, rivets and large screws. Plastic promotionals used the screw-like nails for earlier metal and plastic chassis, augmented with glue on some Chevrolets. Later plastic models would generally use normal screws. Reissues, as noted in the value guide later in this book, typically used plastic pins not found on original issues. (See Notes on Reissues in Section 3.)

Specific delineation of dates in the evolutionary process and design changes could be attempted but would likely prove inaccurate. The reason is that like their toy counterparts, promotionals were not issued as collectibles. In the manufacturing process, substitutions for new production changes did occur chronologically. However, on occasion, regressions to former parts or use of parts intended for other cars (e.g., Studebaker wheels on 1957 Fords) did occur. Likewise, chassis, motor, color and other variables specifically intended for dealership or retail store issues would be used for the other. This may have occurred by accident, due to a temporary parts outage, or simply in a rush to get an order out the door. In such cases common sense should be preferred to hard-and-fast rules.

This Fageol Twin Coach bus by Advance Products Co. is an example of a factory promotional. It was made for Fageol for use by salesmen when contacting potential customers at bus companies.

Consumers Cooperative Association adapted this 1949-65 White 3000 promotional made by Topping for its corporate purposes. The entire truck was molded in white except for the wheel rims which are yellow. It is a very desirable private label version.

This 1955 Buick Roadmaster by Banthrico is a typical bank promotional. It has advertising on the roof that reads: "Finance Your Car At Low Bank Rates and Save Money FARMERS STATE BANK STERLING, KANSAS member F.D.I.C."

Section 3: IDENTIFICATION INFORMATION

Definitions of Terms

The terms promotional and promo are used throughout this book. Further distinctions or descriptions are addressed where they apply. However, the reader should be aware of several definitions, most of which have been used by collectors for many years:

Promotional or **promo** - Any American car or truck made of metal or plastic since 1934 and authorized by the full-sized vehicle manufacturer (i.e., the factory) for promotional purposes. Also, included are some die cast white metal vehicles and several foreign cars by American makers such as Hubley with its rendition of the Triumph TR3. 1/25th was adopted as the standard scale although a few were larger, and many of the earlier pot metal issues were smaller.

Dealer promotional - A promotional believed to have been distributed by a dealership and under the auspices of the factory. Such is determined by an actual factory color and, if plastic, often but not always by the absence of a motor (friction, wind-up, etc.).

Factory promotional - A promotional believed to have been ordered by the factory with distribution primarily made by the factory rather than dealers. These models were used for such purposes as obtaining large contracts, gifts to visiting dignitaries or employee awards.

Friction - A plastic promotional generally of a generic color, with a friction motor and usually sold in retail stores. Note that some dealer promotionals did have friction motors and some had wind-up motors - others, electric or gas. Very few pot metal promotionals had friction motors.

Private label - Advertising information printed on or applied onto a promotional model that is not related to the manufacturer of or to a dealer for the full-sized vehicle or to any color or feature available. Decals, stickers, heat stamping (plastic only) and imprinting were among the methods used for applying the advertisements.

Bank promotional - A promotional containing printed advertising for a financial institution. (At the risk of creating confusion, it should be noted that many promotionals had coin slots and were intended for use as banks.)

Coaster - Any promotional without a motor (e.g., friction or wind-up).

Pot metal often did not allow sufficient detail capabilities to depict very minor changes between model years, if any existed. From 1946 through 1948 the exterior changes in the entire Chrysler Corporation line (i.e., Chrysler, Desoto, Dodge and Plymouth) were somewhere between minimal and nil. For example, the only way to determine if a Dodge was a 1948 model was if the knobs and the steering wheel were a light tan as opposed to the darker tan used for the 1946 and 1947 models. For this reason promotionals such as the pictured 1946-48 Dodge cover multiple model years.

This 1947-49 promotional model of an International model KB phone/utility line truck is difficult to locate. Even more difficult to locate is one with the original boom and utility pole, both of which have been replaced by homemade versions on this example. The white door decals on the International promotional read: "UTILITIES Line Cons't. Co. Inc. JENKINTOWN, PA 744."

Reissue - Models reproduced after their initial issue as promotionals.

Several reference books are readily available for use in the identification of the make, model and year of a car or truck. These books, some of which are dubbed "catalogs" and "spotters' guides" by their publishers, can be very helpful to promotional collectors. Factory literature showing actual colors can be helpful as well; however, collector interest in that regard and sometimes scarcity have made much of that literature quite expensive.

In this text promotionals are identified by make such as Chevrolet and Dodge. Within make, a promotional is further identified by year, body style, series and maker of the promotional. These identifications are defined as follows with the captions as they appear in the value guide listings in Sections 5 and 6:

YEAR - The year of the actual vehicle is listed as opposed to the year the promotional vehicle was issued. The main reason is that design changes, if any, between model years were sometimes too minor to be reflected on the promotional. For example, some of the insignificant differences between full-sized 1951 and 1952 Dodges included a painted lower grill louver and an added red dot reflector on the 1952 model. These items could not be reflected in the promotional.

STYLE - This column contains the body style of the vehicle. The NOTES column may be used to further describe the body style. The abbreviations used for the various body styles under the STYLE column are:

CONV.	convertible or roadster
4DRCONV	four-door convertible
COUPE	business or club coupe
2DRHT	two-door hardtop
4DRHT	four-door hardtop
2DR	two-door sedan
4DR	four-door sedan
2DRWGN	two-door station wagon
4DRWGN	four-door station wagon
AMB	ambulance
BUS	bus
DEL VAN	delivery van
DEMO	demonstration model
DUMP	dump truck
FIRE	fire truck
PANEL	panel truck
PHONE TR	telephone/utility truck
PICKUP	pickup truck
SEMI	semi truck with trailer

Although Jeep station wagons tended to look quite similar for many years, this promotional is a 1949 model as noted by that year on its license plates. This Jeep by Al-Toy is made of sand cast aluminum and measures just under 14½ inches in length. It was cast in several component parts that were then tapped and screwed together. Although it was offered to dealerships, the Jeep was primarily used as a factory promotional for awards and for gifts to visiting dignitaries. Examples with award plaques affixed to the roof have been noted.

With very few exceptions, plastic promotionals were issued in a standard scale of about 1/25th. Pot metal promotionals, again with very few exceptions, were issued in two scales, 1/25th and a second that varied between 1/28th and 1/30th. Pictured for comparison purposes is a 1949 Buick by National Products next to a 1954 Buick by Banthrico. The latter is 1/25th scale and the former, about 1/28th scale.

STAKE	stake truck
TANKER	tank truck
TAXI	taxicab

SERIES - The series name of the vehicle such as Impala and New Yorker, sometimes abbreviated. The use of a series name is especially true for plastic promotionals that were issued when makers produced multiple series of vehicles in a given year. For pot metal promotionals, the series name is listed if determinable. The problem is that exterior series differences between vehicles were often as minor as trim pieces. Such differences were too small or detailed to be reflected on pot metal promotionals.

MAKER - The maker of the promotional model is listed in this column. The makers' names are abbreviated as follows:

ADV	Advance Products Co.
ALTOY	Al-Toy
AMF	AMF Wen-Mac
AMT	AMT Corporation
AUT	Authenticast
BAN	Banthrico
BIRD	Bird
BELL	Bell Products
BUSH	Bush
CRU	Cruver
ELDON	Eldon
ESKA	Eska
GLAD	Gladen
HUB	Hubley
HUD	Hudson (believed to have made some of its own models)
IDEAL	Ideal Models, forerunner of Jo-Han
JOH	Jo-Han
KA	Kaiser (believed to have made some of its own models)
LINC	Lincoln Line
MC	Master Caster
MPC	Model Products Corporation
NP	National Products
PMC	Product Miniature Company
TF	Toy Founders
TOP	Topping
TUCK	Tucker (believed to have made its own models)
SMP	Scale Model Products
UMC	Universal Marketing Co.
UNK	Unknown maker

Collectors are increasingly emphasizing quality, especially if deciding to spend reasonably significant dollars for a promotional. Therefore, accurate assessment of condition or grade is essential because minor differences can mean major dollars. These two 1954 Cadillacs by Banthrico illustrate those minor but expensive differences. The blue Cadillac atop its original box is in **optimal** condition; it is virtually as new looking as the day it was made. The red Cadillac is a very nice and desirable car, but the evident paint chips allow only a **good** condition rating.

Pictured are a pair of 1965 Ford Galaxie 500 promotionals made by AMT. The blue car at the rear is quite nice and would deserve an **optimal** rating. The red car at the front is an unknown because of all the dirt it has accumulated. An optimal, good or even average car may be lurking underneath. Removal of the dirt, a risky process at best, often reveals problems and flaws precluding an optimal rating. Dirty promotionals needing cleaning should not be rated better than **good**.

National Products became a division of Banthrico Industries about 1948 causing some possible confusion for future collectors. Prior to that, National Products' promotionals were smaller than Banthrico's approximately 1/25th scale. They continued to produce the smaller scale models, but entered the larger scale arena with an example being the 1949 Pontiac. About the same time, National Products' markings on vehicles, tires and boxes were not consistent. Vehicles and boxes might be marked National Products Inc. or National Products Div. Others would continue to have National Products markings on their white rubber tires, but their boxes might be issued with a Banthrico stamping.

NOTES - This column identifies special features and any factors that have a positive or negative impact on value. In most instances if there is an impact on the values stated, that impact is noted as a percentage of the values listed and is to be added (+) or subtracted (-) from those values. In other instances, a separate listing is provided with the different values. An example would be uncommon color(s) and/or decals as found on pace cars. For instance, 1957 Thunderbird and 1958 Edsel hardtops are quite common in red and turquoise/white respectively. Therefore, each will have a separate listing for other colors which are much less common and have appreciably higher values.

The AVG., GOOD and OPT. columns are used to present three values for each promotional in conditions from the lowest collectible condition to the highest. <u>Note that vehicles are assumed to be clean. The true condition of those not clean is uncertain because dirt can hide flaws and pose problems during cleaning.</u> (Cleaning requires extreme care and experience; many promotionals have been ruined by improper cleaning.)

The three conditions used are as follows:

AVG. - The amount given is the value of the promotional in average condition. Average condition represents the midpoint in a promotional's state of preservation, a starting point where collectors might begin to consider purchasing a vehicle for their collection. Promotionals in lesser condition are worth much less and might be considered candidates for restoration or use as parts vehicles. Better condition vehicles would be those to which some premium value should be attributed. A promotional in average condition will show definite signs of wear and may have broken, missing or substituted parts that are replaceable.

GOOD - This column contains the value of the promotional in good condition, a condition which is clearly better than average condition. A vehicle in good condition is one that shows minimal evidence of wear and has no broken, missing or incorrect parts.

The 1959 Cadillac Fleetwood by Jo-Han was reissued several years ago. An original red example is pictured next to a reissued white one. Even without looking at the undersides, there are several clues that one is an original and the other is not. The 1959 model tended to warp as illustrated by the red car but not evident with the white. The original had windows that tended to craze as seen on the red Cadillac. The windows on the white car are perfect. Finally, the white Cadillac just looks too new, which it is.

Of all the promotional convertibles ever made, the windshield on this 1949 Packard Custom 8 by Master Caster has to be the most fragile. These Packards are relatively easy to locate without the original windshield. Such cars can never be better that **good.** After all, how realistic is a convertible without its windshield? Examples such as the one pictured with its original windshield are scarce and merit an **optimal** rating providing the other criteria are met as well.

OPT. - The value of the promotional in <u>optimal</u> or virtually perfect condition is given in this column.   Such a vehicle would be one that would be extremely difficult to locate in better condition.

Note that more detailed information concerning condition criteria and its impact on the values of both metal and plastic promotionals is presented in Sections 4 and 5 respectively.

Scarcity and Value

In some ways collectors of promotionals mirror attitudes and preferences of actual vehicle collectors. They are extremely condition conscious preferring their acquisitions to be as nice and original as possible within their means. Both groups demonstrate definite preferences for models of popular cars such as muscle cars and convertibles more than standard models such as sedans.

The prices asked and paid for the popular models have very little relationship to scarcity. Check the values for Corvette promotionals and those for other Chevrolets for the same years. Without actual records, there is no evidence to suggest that significantly fewer Corvette promotionals were issued for any model year. The Corvettes are just that much more popular. The same is true for full-sized cars. For example, about 32% more 1957 Chevrolets were made than 1954 models, yet 1957 models are much more valued today than the 1954's.

A clarifying comment is needed at this juncture. Scarcity is a much greater factor in collecting pot metal promotionals than plastic ones. For example, unless it is a scarcer vehicle, a pot metal Ford or Chevrolet will not command a higher price than an Oldsmobile. Pot metal convertibles are highly sought items not only because they are more popular but also because they are scarce. Comparatively few convertibles were made and most found are broken.

Notes on Reissues

One indication of the popularity (and, thereby the profit potential) of any given collectible hobby is the introduction of reproductions or, as referred to in this text, reissues. Unfortunately for some, reissues of promotionals were introduced several years ago and continue today. For persons merely seeking a decent example of a specific full-sized vehicle, reissues may be suitable. For most others seeking original examples, reissues are other than beneficial, especially when offered by sellers as originals and acquired in error by collectors.

There are several ways to differentiate between an original and a reissue pot metal promotional. Most would require detailed descriptions that are not necessary if the observer

The 1959 Desoto by Jo-Han has been reissued; however, the one pictured above is an original vehicle. The window crazing is one of many factors that permit this determination. However, the relative values involved, $100 vs. $35, represent only a potential $65 error. Such an error can be much greater. Pictured below are two 1970 Corvette promotionals; both are very desirable vehicles. However, a reissue of the coupe has been produced. Given that the original is worth about $400 and the reissue only about $20, considerable caution should be exercised when purchasing one of these cars. A $380 error can affect a lot of wallets.

simply examines the paint. The trim including windows and bumpers on pot metal promotionals was not masked off. Rather, templates were used generally resulting in a minor feathering look in such areas. If there is any masking as evidenced by raised paint edges, the vehicle is either a reissue or a repaint. Refer to the value guide section for pot metal promotionals later in this book for models known to have been reissued.

Several factors should be noted about reissued plastic promotionals. Not all factors are true for all reissues, but all should be considered when evaluating a promotional. These factors include:

- Vehicles originally made of warping plastic are reissued in nonwarping plastic.

- Reissues of vehicles originally having metal bumpers have plastic bumpers.

- Windows that are typically crazed (a hazing condition possibly caused by heat and/or age) are unusually clear.

- Originally friction-powered vehicles in reissue form are coasters with no chassis provision for the motor.

- Plastic pins are used to attach the chassis and body.

- Color(s), especially on two-tone vehicles, are unusually vivid and not ones typically found on that year and make of promotional.

- The original box, if present, does not have the original maker identification.

Promotionals known to have been reissued are identified in the value guide listings that appear in Sections 4 and 5 of this book. Other reissues are certain to exist or appear in the future. Sellers, especially auctions with the inherent anonymity of the consignor, have been noted for selling reissues as originals. A purchasing error, buying a reissue assuming it was an original, can result in a several hundred-dollar loss. If only for that reason, a familiarity with the above factors and with the known reissues is a prudent precaution before spending significant dollars on promotionals.

During the 1930's National Products issued a few pot metal promotional models in a scale of about 1/12th. The larger vehicles such as this 1937-40 International model D panel truck were excessively susceptible to breakage resulting in few survivors for collectors today.

These two 1935 Studebaker Presidents by National Products illustrate the difference between the larger scale and smaller, standard scale for pot metal promotionals of the 1930's. The larger is a regular sedan and the smaller is their Land Cruiser version.

The following two Oldsmobiles illustrate the lack of proportional consistency with pot metal:

1953 Oldsmobile 88 by Banthrico

1954 Oldsmobile 88 by Banthrico

Although a few promotionals were made of cast aluminum and die cast white metal, pot metal was the dominant material used for metal promotionals. This started with the 1934 Studebaker and continued until about 1956, about seven years after plastic promotionals were introduced in 1949. A few pot metal promotionals were issued after 1956. The last was Banthrico's 1967 Willys M-715 U.S. Army stake truck, a factory promotional produced in concert with attempts to secure a military production contract.

Pot metal promotionals were intended to be accurate, scale renditions of real vehicles. They were issued in several scales from about 1/12th to about 1/30th. Of these, the largest issues such as the 1935 Studebaker and the 1934 through 1940 Internationals are among the most scarce and, thus, more valuable due primarily to their susceptibility to breakage. Issues of about 1/25th scale, as with later plastic issues, are the most prevalent scale. Adherence to scale was not always consistent. Some larger cars such as Oldsmobiles may seem smaller or the same size as typically smaller cars such as Ramblers.

Consistency of vehicle proportions also varied. Some renditions were excellent while others were considerably less so. Oldsmobiles again provide examples of this factor. The 1953 Oldsmobile has excellent proportions resulting in a very real look. By comparison, the 1954 Oldsmobile looks considerably out of proportion. Proportional inaccuracy was the product of mold design but was also probably affected by the pot metal production process as well. Certainly, the latter impacted the degree to which design details could be incorporated. As a result, details were often distorted or omitted. However, some early promotionals did have tires marked "Firestone," but thereafter the tires and wheels used were never realistic.

Despite the fact that pot metal promotionals sometimes lacked proper proportions and frequently omitted design details, they were and continue to be very popular among toy consumers of the period and collectors today. Part of that popularity is attributable to their toy-like appeal. Also, pot metal promotionals offer collectors models of vehicles such as Packards, Mercurys, Nashes, Studebakers and others seldom available in other forms.

Three problems are notable for pot metal promotionals:

■ Paint - The paint did not always adhere properly and could easily be chipped. In some cases paint adherence problems seem more severe than with others, the 1954 Lincoln for example. Some mint/boxed examples of originals never before unwrapped are found with minor paint chips.

As depicted in the above photo, pot metal promotionals were close but not accurate renditions of the actual full-size vehicles. Nor were the colors used always the correct shade. Note that the 1951 Ford F-1 panel truck by National Products is typical of a pot metal promotional in **average condition**.

These two 1953 Ford Customline sedans by Banthrico are examples of pot metal promotionals in good and optimal conditions. The Ford pictured on its box is virtually perfect with no paint loss and is in **optimal condition**. The second example has some paint chipping, which is most evident above the windshield, and would rate in **good condition**.

■ Distortion - The die design sometimes resulted in distortions, probably during the cooling process, that became inherent to specific models.

■ Metal fatigue - The pot metal alloy may have been poor resulting in metal fatigue to appear and increase over time, often to the point of self-destruction. This type of problem, which is also found in die cast white metal toys of the era, is not generally inherent to any specific issue.

These problems augmented by the need for more adherence to scale and accuracy resulted in the replacement of pot metal by plastic as the material of choice for promotionals by 1956.

Condition Criteria

The following guidelines apply to metal promotionals and should be considered when using the value guide that follows in this section:

Average Condition (AVG.) - A vehicle in average condition is one which represents a minimal level of collectibility. Examples in lesser condition have negligible value except for parts or as candidates for restoration. A vehicle in average condition is one that has:

■ at least 60% of the original paint or virtually 100% paint for a repaint of professional quality using the correct color(s)
■ no sign of repair
■ minimal signs of metal fatigue
■ no damage
■ no severe wear

Good Condition (GOOD) - The appearance of a vehicle in good condition is of such quality that it would be easily acceptable by most collectors. An example in good condition should have:

■ at least 85% of the original paint, no repainting
■ no sign of repair
■ no replacement parts
■ no sign of metal fatigue
■ no damage
■ minimal wear

Optimal Condition (OPT.) - An optimal vehicle is a candidate for the best of collections and is in a condition that is extremely difficult to locate. Such a promotional should have:

1948-49 Hudson Commodore by Master Caster in two-tone. This car came with and without whitewall tires. Less common solid color versions including a very few with friction motors were also made and possibly issued only for 1949.

1954 Chevrolet 210 by Banthrico with box

1947-48 Buick Super by National Products with box

1953-54 Nash Rambler by Banthrico with advertising on its roof that reads: "When I'm Full of Money Drive me To The MERIDEN PERMANENT BUILDING AND LOAN ASSOCIATION 61-63 COLONY ST. MERIDEN, CONNECTICUT"

- virtually all of its original paint (about 98%) with no touch-up or repainting
- no sign of repair
- no replacement parts
- no sign of metal fatigue
- no damage
- virtually no wear

Value Considerations

The condition criteria described previously represent the primary factors that determine the value of a metal promotional. In addition, there are several other factors that need to be considered when determining value as follows:

- Add 20% for two-tone paint - Two-tone paint is uncommon on dealer promotionals except for the 1948-49 Hudson where solid colors are less common.

- Add 20% for the original box - Most original boxes for pot metal promotionals were made of plain, tan cardboard with minimal markings including some handwritten designations. However, they are scarce and should be both in good shape and correspond to the vehicle in regard to make, model, year and color as applicable. Discretion and common sense are needed concerning boxes because makers such as National Products did not always mark boxes in a consistent or even accurate manner. Some vehicles, especially trucks, were made with National Products markings and issued in Banthrico boxes. The 1952 Ford and 1949-53 Studebaker pickups are examples.

- Add $5 for the original key for bank models - The key is generally missing and should result in no deduction.

- Advertising - The advertisements which may appear on a metal promotional are too varied to specify an added value or percentage. To be of increased value, the advertising must have a generally universal appeal. Advertising for a local dealership or financial institution might have an added value that is limited to persons in that locale. In contrast, a vehicle with advertising that promotes a product or service such as a moving company can appeal to multiple groups of collectors. Such advertising increases the demand and reduces the supply of promotionals available to collectors with the expected reflection on value.

- Distortion - This factor is generally inherent to specific pot metal promotionals and is reflected in the values presented. No deduction should be made unless encountered in a model for which distortion is uncommon.

This 1952 Ford F-2 stake truck is bronze plated. Painted versions are more realistic and, therefore, preferred by collectors to plated vehicles.

Chevrolet made minimal design changes between their 1949 and 1950 model years. On the left is a 1950 and on the right is a 1949, both by Banthrico. Note the lower, vertical grill bars on the 1949.

Vehicle identification reference books are helpful for determining model years for the above Chevrolets and for these two Studebakers. The National Products 1947-48 example is on the left and their 1949 example on the right. The only notable difference is the spacing between the horizontal grill sections.

■ Paint - Templates were used for masking out borders or design details on pot metal promotionals. No deduction should be made for the often indistinct borders or for moderate flaws in the original paint. Many pot metal promotionals have been repainted during their lives. If not repainted correctly with original car colors, their values are seriously impacted. Deduct at least 50% from the average value (AVG.) if the quality of the repaint is poor and/or nonoriginal colors are used. In contrast, a properly repainted model using correct paint is worth approximately the same as a model in average collectible condition.

■ Plating - Deduct 20% for pot metal promotionals that are bronzed or plated as opposed to painted.

■ Breaks or damage - Promotionals with significant problems such as missing windshields or bottoms, breaks, repairs and the like should generally be avoided.

The preceding condition criteria and value considerations are intended to assist the collector, owner, buyer, seller, appraiser, etc. of pot metal promotionals in accurately evaluating vehicles. There seems to be a tendency to avoid reading and to rush directly to the value guide to see what an item is worth. There is also an optimistic tendency, especially on the part of owners and sellers, to overrate their item(s) and look only at the highest values provided. Impatience and optimism can result in judgement errors measured in significant dollars. This is because collectors of pot metal promotionals are very condition conscious. The values provided in the listing that follows can be of considerable assistance. This is especially true if the user does his or her reading beforehand and properly evaluates the condition of the vehicle(s) being checked.

The Willys model M-274 "Mechanical Mule" by Al-Toy was a factory promotional used for a U.S. Army contract. It was not available from Willys dealerships. The mule was intended for hauling supplies and ammunition to the front lines. When under enemy fire, the controls were designed to allow the operator to drive the vehicle in reverse while crawling on the ground at its front.

1950 Buick Super by National Products

1952 Cadillac 62 by Banthrico

1950 Chevrolet Styleline convertible by Banthrico

1953 Chevrolet 210 by Banthrico

1955 Chrysler New Yorker by Banthrico

1949 Desoto Custom by National Products

◆◆ METAL PROMOTIONALS ◆◆

YEAR	STYLE	SERIES	MAKER	NOTES	AVG.	GOOD	OPT.
▼▼▼ BUICK ▼▼▼							
1939	4DR	SUPER	NP		400	750	1000
1940	4DR	SUPER	NP		425	800	1250
1941	4DR	CENTURY	NP	FASTBACK	425	800	1250
1946	4DR	SUPER	NP		200	300	650
1947-48	4DR	SUPER	NP		90	250	400
1949	4DR	SUPER	NP		90	200	350
1950	4DR	SUPER	NP	-40% IF ON BASE	90	225	375
1952	4DR	ROADMASTER	BAN		75	150	300
1953	4DR	ROADMASTER	BAN		75	150	300
1954	2DRHT	ROADMASTER	BAN	REISSUE EXISTS	125	225	400
1955	2DRHT	ROADMASTER	BAN		90	300	425
1956	4DRHT	SUPER	BAN		90	300	425
▼▼▼ CADILLAC ▼▼▼							
1952	4DR	62	BAN		75	135	250
1954	4DR	FLEETWOOD	BAN	REISSUE EXISTS	90	165	300
1955	4DR	FLEETWOOD	BAN		90	200	325
1956	2DRHT	BIARRITZ	BAN	REISSUE EXISTS	90	225	350
▼▼▼ CHEVROLET ▼▼▼							
1947	2DR	FLEETLINE	NP	FASTBACK, AERO SEDAN	100	250	375
1948	2DR	FLEETLINE	NP	FASTBACK, AERO SEDAN	125	275	400
1949	2DR	FLEETLINE	BAN	FASTBACK	125	275	400
1949	2DR	STYLELINE	BAN		125	250	375
1949	4DR	FLEETLINE	BAN	FASTBACK	125	250	375
1949	4DR	STYLELINE	BAN		125	250	375
1949	COUPE	STYLELINE	BAN		125	250	375
1949	CONV.	STYLELINE	BAN	ALL VERSIONS	150	275	400
1950	2DR	FLEETLINE	BAN	FASTBACK	200	375	500
1950	2DR	STYLELINE	BAN		75	175	275
1950	2DRHT	STYLELINE	BAN		75	175	275
1950	4DR	FLEETLINE	BAN	FASTBACK	75	200	300
1950	4DR	STYLELINE	BAN		75	175	275
1950	COUPE	STYLELINE	BAN		75	175	275
1950	CONV.	STYLELINE	BAN		100	225	325
1953	4DR	210	BAN		125	250	400
1954	CONV.	CORVETTE	BAN	CIRCA 1973, WHITE, RED OR BLUE	75	175	275
1954	4DR	210	BAN		40	75	125
1955	2DRHT	BEL AIR	BAN	REISSUE EXISTS	90	175	275
1956	2DRHT	210	BAN		90	175	250
					90	175	250
▼▼▼ CHRYSLER ▼▼▼							
1934	4DR	AIRFLOW	NP		300	600	850
1946	4DR	NEW YORKER	NP	METAL HUBS, FIRESTONE TIRES	75	125	175
1947-48	4DR	NEW YORKER	NP		65	100	165
1949	4DR	NEW YORKER	NP		90	200	325
1950	4DR	NEW YORKER	BAN	ALL VERSIONS	90	175	300
1953	2DRHT	NEW YORKER	BAN		90	175	375
1954	4DR	NEW YORKER	BAN		175	300	450
1955	4DR	NEW YORKER	BAN	REISSUE EXISTS	90	200	375
1955	4DR	NEW YORKER	BAN	DEALER OR COLOR MARKINGS	110	240	450
▼▼▼ DESOTO ▼▼▼							
1946-48	4DR	CUSTOM	NP		100	250	400
1949	4DR	CUSTOM	NP		90	200	325

1951-52 Dodge Coronet by Banthrico

1954 Dodge Royal by Banthrico

1948-50 Dodge model B stake by National Products

Indiana State Police 1948 Ford by Master Caster

1956 Ford Customline by Banthrico

1952 Ford F-1 pickup by National Products

YEAR	STYLE	SERIES	MAKER	NOTES	AVG.	GOOD	OPT.
▼▼▼ DIAMOND T TRUCKS ▼▼▼							
1935	STAKE		NP	LARGE SCALE	1500	3000	4500
▼▼▼ DODGE ▼▼▼							
1946-48	4DR	CUSTOM	NP		75	100	175
1949	4DR	CORONET	NP		90	200	325
1950	4DR	CORONET	BAN	ALL VERSIONS	90	165	300
1951-52	4DR	CORONET	BAN		75	165	300
1953	4DR	CORONET	BAN		90	150	300
1954	4DR	ROYAL	BAN		100	250	375
▼▼▼ DODGE TRUCKS ▼▼▼							
1948-50	PICKUP	B	NP		125	275	400
1948-50	STAKE	B	NP	+10% FOR PRINTED SIGN BOARDS	150	275	400
▼▼▼ FAGEOL BUS ▼▼▼							
1950-53	BUS	TWIN COACH	ADV		175	400	525
▼▼▼ FARGO TRUCKS ▼▼▼							
1948-50	PICKUP		NP		150	400	500
1948-50	STAKE		NP		150	400	500
▼▼▼ FEDERAL TRUCKS ▼▼▼							
1936	TANKER		NP		600	800	1000
▼▼▼ FORD ▼▼▼							
1946	4DR	SUPER DELUXE	AMT	DIE CAST, ALSO REPRESENTS EARLY 1947	90	125	175
1948	2DR	SUPER DELUXE	MC	ALSO REPRESENTS LATE 1947, +30% FOR FRICTION	90	150	200
1948	2DR	SUPER DELUXE	MC	TAXI, FIRE, ARMY & GENERIC POLICE	100	225	300
1948	2DR	SUPER DELUXE	MC	TAXI, FIRE, ARMY & GENERIC POLICE WITH FRICTION	115	265	365
1948	2DR	SUPER DELUXE	MC	SPECIFIC POLICE AGENCY, +20% FOR FRICTION	115	265	365
1948	2DR	SUPER DELUXE	MC	SELFRIDGE AIR FORCE BASE, +20% FOR FRICTION	115	265	365
1950	2DR	CUSTOM	MC		100	175	265
1950	2DR	CUSTOM	MC	TAXI, POLICE & FIRE	100	250	350
1950	4DR	CUSTOM	BAN		90	125	225
1953	4DR	CUSTOMLINE	BAN		90	150	265
1955	4DR	FAIRLANE	BAN	REISSUE EXISTS	90	150	285
1956	4DR	CUSTOMLINE	BAN		100	200	300
▼▼▼ FORD TRUCKS ▼▼▼							
1948-50	PANEL	F-1	NP		125	250	375
1948-50	PICKUP	F-1	NP		125	250	350
1948-50	STAKE	F-2	NP		225	375	550
1951	PANEL	F-1	NP		200	350	475
1951	PICKUP	F-1	NP		200	350	450
1951	STAKE	F-2	NP		200	350	475
1952	PANEL	F-1	NP		125	250	375
1952	PICKUP	F-1	NP		125	250	350
1952	STAKE	F-2	NP		125	250	375
1953	PICKUP	F-100	BAN	REISSUE EXISTS	100	225	350

1948-50 GMC model FC pickup by National Products

1951 Hudson Commodore by Master Caster

1954 Hudson Hornet by Master Caster

1953 Kaiser Manhattan by Banthrico

1951 Lincoln Cosmopolitan by Banthrico

1954 Mercury Monterey by Banthrico

❖❖ METAL PROMOTIONALS ❖❖

YEAR	STYLE	SERIES	MAKER	NOTES	AVG.	GOOD	OPT.
▼▼▼ GRAHAM ▼▼▼							
1934	4DR		NP		500	750	1250
▼▼▼ GMC TRUCKS ▼▼▼							
1948-50	PICKUP	FC	NP	-40% IF ON BASE	90	150	225
1948-50	DUMP	FF	NP	-40% IF ON BASE	125	200	265
1954	PICKUP	100	NP	-40% IF ON BASE	125	225	300
1954	DUMP	350	NP	-40% IF ON BASE	150	275	350
1958	PICKUP		BUSH		100	175	250
1959	PICKUP		BUSH		100	175	250
▼▼▼ HUDSON ▼▼▼							
1934	4DR	TERRAPLANE	NP		500	700	1000
1948-49	4DR	COMMODORE	MC	2-TONE, WITH OR WITHOUT WHITEWALLS	150	250	325
1948-49	4DR	COMMODORE	MC	SOLID COLOR, BLACKWALLS, +40% FOR FRICTION	135	225	300
1948-49	4DR	COMMODORE	MC	YELLOW CAB	250	350	425
1950	4DR	COMMODORE	MC		225	350	450
1951	4DR	COMMODORE	MC		150	275	350
1954	4DR	HORNET	MC		300	475	650
1955	4DR	HORNET	MC		350	750	1000
▼▼▼ INTERNATIONAL TRUCKS ▼▼▼							
1934-36	PANEL	C	NP	LARGE SCALE	900	2200	3000
1937-40	PANEL	D	NP	LARGE SCALE	900	2200	3000
1947	PHONE TR	KB	NP	1/30TH, -20% FOR MISSING BOOM AND POLE	200	375	550
1961-71	CONV.	SCOUT	ESKA		50	100	150
▼▼▼ KAISER ▼▼▼							
1946	BUS	KAISER COACH	KA	SAND CAST ALUMINUM, 8-WHEEL, ARTICULATED	750	1250	1650
1953	4DR	MANHATTAN	BAN	ALL VERSIONS	200	350	450
▼▼▼ LINCOLN ▼▼▼							
1949	4DR	COSMOPOLITAN	NP		150	275	400
1950	4DR	COSMOPOLITAN	NP		200	450	600
1951	4DR	COSMOPOLITAN	BAN		125	275	350
1953	4DR	COSMOPOLITAN	BAN		275	350	450
1954	2DRHT	COSMOPOLITAN	BAN	REISSUE EXISTS	90	200	300
▼▼▼ MACK TRUCKS ▼▼▼							
1940-53	TANKER	L	NP		150	275	375
▼▼▼ MERCURY ▼▼▼							
1940	4DR		UNK	DIE CAST, BANK/STAMP DISPENSER	20	40	80
1949	4DR		NP		100	275	400
1950	4DR		NP		200	350	500
1950	4DR		NP	PACE CAR MARKINGS ON ROOF	225	375	550
1951	4DR		BAN		150	200	325
1953	4DR	MONTEREY	BAN	HAS 1952 DECK LID	200	350	450
1954	2DRHT	MONTEREY	BAN	REISSUE EXISTS	100	200	325
1955	2DRHT	MONTEREY	BAN		150	325	425

1950 Nash Statesman by National Products

1953 Packard Clipper by Banthrico

1946-48 Plymouth Spec. Deluxe by National Products

1953 & 1955 Plymouths by Banthrico

1949 Pontiac Chieftain by National Products

1953 Studebaker Commander by Banthrico

✦✦ METAL PROMOTIONALS ✦✦

YEAR	STYLE	SERIES	MAKER	NOTES	AVG.	GOOD	OPT.
▾▾▾ NASH ▾▾▾							
1949	4DR	600	NP	+20% FOR 2-TONE	75	100	200
1950	4DR	STATESMAN	NP	+20% FOR 2-TONE, SOME HAVE "49" ON BOTTOM	75	100	200
1950-52	CONV.	RAMBLER	NP		100	325	500
1951-52	2DRHT	RAMBLER	BAN	+20% FOR 2-TONE	75	200	375
1953-54	2DRHT	RAMBLER	BAN	+20% FOR 2-TONE	75	200	375
▾▾▾ OLDSMOBILE ▾▾▾							
1953	4DR	88	BAN		125	300	425
1954	2DRHT	88	BAN	REISSUE EXISTS	90	150	300
1955	2DRHT	98	BAN		325	400	500
▾▾▾ PACKARD ▾▾▾							
1949	CONV.	CUSTOM 8	MC	-50% FOR MISSING ORIG. WINDSHIELD	150	300	500
1953	4DR	CLIPPER	BAN	REISSUE EXISTS, +20% FOR 2-TONE	100	225	400
1954	4DR	CLIPPER	BAN	+20% FOR 2-TONE	250	375	500
▾▾▾ PLYMOUTH ▾▾▾							
1946-48	4DR	SPEC. DELUXE	NP		100	200	325
1953	4DR	CRANBROOK	BAN		100	165	275
1955	2DR	BELVEDERE	BAN		100	200	375
1956	2DR	SAVOY	BAN		100	200	350
▾▾▾ PONTIAC ▾▾▾							
1948	4DR	STREAMLINER	NP	FASTBACK	75	115	185
1949	4DR	CHIEFTAIN	NP		90	175	285
1953	2DRHT	CHIEFTAIN	BAN	REISSUE EXISTS	90	200	300
1955	2DRHT	STAR CHIEF	BAN		125	275	375
▾▾▾ REO ▾▾▾							
1936	4DR		NP		500	775	1150
1937	TANKER		NP		500	775	1150
▾▾▾ STUDEBAKER ▾▾▾							
1934	4DR	PRESIDENT	NP	LOUVERS: '34 VERTICAL, '34½ HORIZONTAL	200	325	425
1935	4DR	PRESIDENT	NP	SMALLER SCALE, BOTH VERSIONS	400	750	1150
1935	4DR	PRESIDENT	NP	LARGER SCALE	1500	2500	3500
1936	4DR	PRESIDENT	NP	APPROX. 4½ INCHES	150	350	485
1936	4DR	PRESIDENT	NP	APPROX. 6½ INCHES, BOTH VERSIONS	325	550	800
1938	4DR	COMMANDER	NP		500	800	1000
1947-48	2DR	COMMANDER	NP		100	150	265
1949	2DR	COMMANDER	NP		100	150	265
1953	2DRHT	COMMANDER	BAN		225	350	425
▾▾▾ STUDEBAKER TRUCKS ▾▾▾							
1934	STAKE	T	NP		400	750	1250
1949-53	PICKUP	2R	NP		175	275	375
1949-53	STAKE	2R	NP		200	350	475

1949-53 Studebaker 2R pickup by National Products

1941-42 White Horse van by National Products

1949-65 White 3000 stake by National Products

1949 Willys Jeep CJ-3A fire truck by Al-Toy

1959-63 Willys station wagon by Authenticast

1961 Willys Jeep Surrey by Authenticast

✦✦ METAL PROMOTIONALS ✦✦

YEAR	STYLE	SERIES	MAKER	NOTES	AVG.	GOOD	OPT.
▾▾▾ TUCKER ▾▾▾							
1948	4DR		TUCK	REAR SKIRTS OUTLINED, REISSUE EXISTS	450	800	1150
1948	4DR		TUCK	REAR SKIRTS OUTLINED W/ ASHTRAY BASE	550	900	1250
1948	4DR		TUCK	REAR SKIRTS NOT OUTLINED	500	850	1200
1948	4DR		TUCK	REAR SKIRTS NOT OUTLINED W/ ASHTRAY BASE	600	1000	1350
▾▾▾ WHITE TRUCKS ▾▾▾							
1936-40	STAKE		NP	MARKED "FIRST STREAMLINED TRUCK"	225	325	550
1939-40	DEL VAN	WHITE HORSE	NP	POP-OUT ENGINE	225	375	575
1941-42	DEL VAN	WHITE HORSE	NP	POP-OUT ENGINE	250	400	600
1941	STAKE		NP	FEATURES LOW HEADLIGHTS	250	375	575
1949-65	STAKE	3000	NP	CABOVER MODEL WITH ENGINE	200	275	400
▾▾▾ WILLYS & JEEP ▾▾▾							
1946-49	PICKUP		ALTOY	12", SAND CAST ALUMINUM, ALL VERSIONS	175	350	575
1949	CONV.	JEEPSTER	ALTOY	15 1/4", SAND CAST ALUMINUM	900	1750	2500
1949	2DRWGN		ALTOY	14 ½", SAND CAST ALUMINUM"	750	1400	1900
1949	FIRE	CJ-3A	ALTOY	12", SAND CAST ALUMINUM"	1500	2250	3850
1949	FLATBED	M-274	ALTOY	ARMY "MECHANICAL MULE," 10 ½"	400	625	900
1950	2DRWGN		BAN	. . . .	225	375	450
1957-63	PICKUP	FC-170	BUSH	1/25TH	100	175	275
1957-63	PICKUP	FC-170	AUT	1/20TH	125	185	300
1957-63	STAKE	FC-170	AUT	1/20TH	150	225	325
1957-63	STAKE	FC-170	AUT	1/20TH, U.S. POST OFFICE MARKINGS	165	275	375
1959-63	2DRWGN		AUT	. . . .	100	200	300
1961	CONV.	SURREY	AUT	+10% FOR "RENT-A-JEEP GALA"	50	75	125
1967	STAKE	M-715	BAN	U.S. ARMY WITH CAB TOP UP	75	125	165

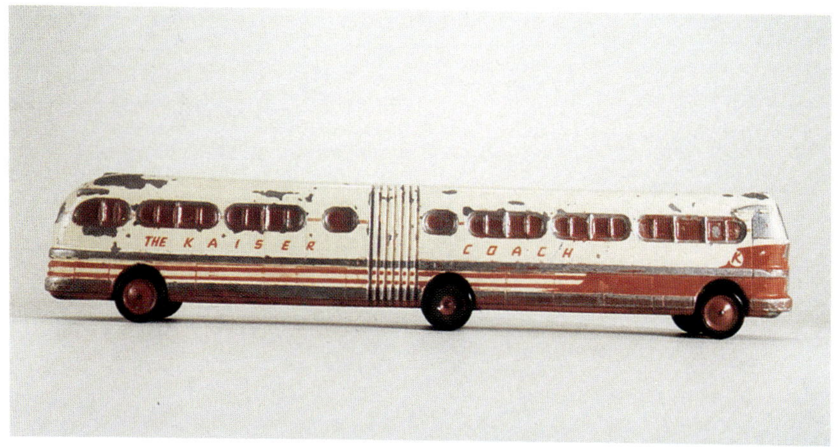

In 1946 the Permanente Metals Corporation, a division of Kaiser Industries, built one sixty foot, articulated bus for use by Trailways. It was powered by a six-cylinder Cummings diesel. The company also produced this factory promotional using the Trailways color scheme but with Kaiser markings instead. Few, if any, promotionals are more scarce than this bus.

BRAND NEW, GRAND NEW
1950 **DODGE** MINIATURES!

AUTHENTIC ALL METAL SCALE MODELS
WITH RUBBER TIRES -- ACTUAL 1950 COLORS
IMPRINTED* IN BULK WITH FIRM NAME

Large and distinctive — 8 inches long!

ORDER 1950 **DODGE** MINIATURES HERE—DETACH AND MAIL TODAY!

National **PRODUCTS DIVISION**
17 NORTH DESPLAINES STREET, CHICAGO 6, ILLINOIS

DATE_________________

QUANTITY	ITEM	PRICE	TOTAL
(In Bulk)	**DODGE MINIATURES IN BULK.** Packed in assortment of ALL DODGE colors. If imprinting is desired show exact wording in box on right.	@______	
(Color Line Sets)	**DODGE COLOR LINE SETS.** 14 Dodge miniatures, each finished in a different new 1950 color. Names of colors are imprinted on roof for easy identification.	**$18.50** per set	
(Display Cabinets)	**DISPLAY CABINET** for the DODGE Color Line Set. Constructed of heavy plate glass with wood base and sliding doors in back. Packed completely assembled, ready to use. Size 20" high, 22½" wide, 10" deep.	**$27.95**	
	IMPRINTING bulk miniatures in quantities of less than 100	**$7.50**	
	For Illinois shipments add 2%; for Ohio 3%		
		$________	

BULK PRICES

Lots of	1-99	100	200	500	1000-Up
EACH	$1.30*	1.20	1.17	1.14	1.12

* Imprinting furnished FREE on orders for 100 or more DODGE Miniatures. For imprinting less than 100 add $7.50 to total cost of order.

ALL SHIPMENTS F.O.B. CHICAGO.

IMPRINTING ON BULK MINIATURES

Type or Print exact wording desired.

____

____

____

Note — Color Line Sets CANNOT be imprinted with firm name.

Please enter our order for DODGE Miniatures as specified above. Enclosed is our check for $__________in full payment, or as a deposit, balance to be paid c.o.d.

Firm Name_________________________________ Address_________________________________

City_________________________ Zone_______ State___________ By_________________________

TERMS — FULL PAYMENT WITH ORDER OR 25% WITH ORDER, BALANCE C.O.D.

ALL SHIPMENTS F.O.B. CHICAGO.

SHIPMENTS MADE TO COINCIDE WITH ANNOUNCEMENT!

These two 1950 Dodge Coronets were ordered from National Products in the summer of 1949 using the order form that appears on the opposing page. The acquisition of National Products by Banthrico was in the offing and a transition was in process. When delivered, the one on the left was devoid of either company's markings and had no bank slot on the underside. The example on the right has both Banthrico and National Products identification on the underside.

Based on the order form, these 1950 Dodge promotionals could be ordered:

- With no printing (Printing was free when 100 or more cars were ordered; otherwise, the cost was $7.50 per order.)
- With dealer advertising imprinted on roofs
- In a group of 14 colors with color names imprinted on roofs

This group of eight 1950 Chevrolets by Banthrico was obtained from the same dealership. They are painted in factory colors with the colors printed on their roofs as follows:

Styleline coupe - Rodeo Beige　　　　　Styleline coupe - Falcon Grey/Grecian Grey
Styleline 2dr - Crystal Green　　　　　Styleline 2dr - Grecian Grey
Styleline 4dr - Oxford Maroon　　　　　Styleline 4dr - Crystal Green/Mist Green
Fleetline 2dr - Maryland Black　　　　　Fleetline 4dr - Falcon Green

This 1949 Oldsmobile 98 by Cruver was one of the first plastic promotionals and was offered in three colors, Crest Blue (pictured), Tawnee Buff and Sea Foam Green on the original order form. All of the bright trim pieces were applied as opposed to being molded-in. As such, it is one of the most detailed promotionals ever made. The original box is very scarce.

Red 1970 Pontiac GTO's were used in a large scale promotional program. Those GTO's had a Michigan license plate and no tach on the hood like the car on the left. The less common dealership promotional on the right had "1970" on the license plate and a hood tach.

Soon after World War II toy makers recognized the advantages that plastic offered as compared to other materials such as cast iron, steel and slush metal, which was also known as pot metal. Naturally, plastic was soon tried and successfully adapted for the manufacture of promotionals. Some of the first plastic promotionals include:

> 1949 Ford by AMT
> 1948-49 Hudson attributed to Hudson
> 1947-49 International pickup by PMC
> 1949-50 Kaiser by Toy Founders
> 1949 Oldsmobile by Cruver
> 1949 Plymouth by AMT

Despite the advantages permitted by plastic such as better detail, adherence to scale, probable reduction in production costs, increased color versatility and more, plastic promotionals shared the market with those made of pot metal through 1956. Thereafter, the vast majority of promotionals were made of plastic. Gone was the toy-like look replaced by the realism of scale models.

Although plastic would replace pot metal, the material was not without its own set of problems that included:

■ Surface rub - Plastic promotionals with some exceptions (e.g., Chevrolets until 1958) were individually packaged in cardboard boxes. If not carefully wrapped, a vehicle could slide around inside creating rub marks primarily on the roof. A similar situation occurs with the chrome plating on plastic bumpers at the center and ends.

■ Warpage - Irregularly over the first fourteen or so years, some companies issued promotionals that would contort, especially if exposed to heat. Like distortion in pot metal promotionals, warpage was inherent to specific plastic models. However, warpage occurred over time and could be minimized by control of environmental conditions, especially heat.

■ Breakage - When subjected to pressure or forceful contact, plastic is clearly susceptible to breakage. The most notable areas are the windshield posts, wing vent posts, sun visors (on convertibles) and applied trim parts such as hood ornaments. Windshield posts and wing vent posts are also susceptible to

The two cars presented on this page are examples of "mint/boxed" or "new/boxed" promotionals that are not as mint or new as they should be. Rather, they cannot be valued as **optimal** cars because of problems. They also serve as examples of why original, boxed plastic promotionals should be carefully examined prior to purchase.

This 1964 Chrysler 300 by Jo-Han is beginning to demonstrate the downward warpage starting above the front wheel wells. Such warpage is typical for this vehicle.   This Chrysler is rated and valued as **good** despite being "new-in-the-box."

A similar example is this 1971 Dodge Charger RT by MPC. It was found still wrapped in its original box with decals inside at a defunct Dodge dealership in November 1996. A careful examination spotted a cracked right roof support that relegates the car to **average** plus added value for the pristine box and unapplied decals.

bowing when pressure is applied but not enough to cause breakage.

■ Window distortion - The clear plastic used in some of the mid-to-late 1950's vehicles might exhibit two types of problems. Some would develop a glazed or crazing look. Others might tend to ripple and bow outward.

Each of the above potential problems reduces the value of a plastic promotional as will be noted in the narrative that follows. Unfortunately, each of the above may also be found on some "mint/boxed" examples never previously unwrapped. Therefore, caution should be exercised even when considering so-called "mint/boxed" plastic promotionals.

Condition Criteria

The following guidelines apply to plastic promotionals and should be considered when using the value guide that follows in this section:

<u>Average Condition (AVG.)</u> - A vehicle in average condition is one which represents a minimal level of collectibility. Examples in lesser condition have negligible value except for parts or as candidates for restoration. A vehicle in average condition is one that may have:

■ significant areas of surface abrasion such as scratches and like problems
■ significant surface rub(s)
■ minor damage that can be or has been repaired and repainted
■ no broken or missing parts that cannot be replaced
■ moderate warpage and only if typical for the vehicle
■ no severe wear

<u>Good Condition (GOOD)</u> - The appearance of a vehicle in good condition is of such quality that it would be easily acceptable by most collectors. An example in good condition should have:

■ only minor areas of surface abrasion
■ only minor areas of surface rub
■ no repair or repainting
■ no broken or missing parts
■ minimal wear
■ minor bowing, if any, of windshield or wing vent posts
■ minor warpage and only if typical for the vehicle

<u>Optimal Condition (OPT.)</u> - An optimal vehicle is a candidate for the best of collections and is in a condition upon which it would be extremely difficult to

Boxes add value to a promotional, and some boxes add more interest than others. The box that accompanies the 1961 Chevrolet Corvair above is rather plain with only the make and color stamped on the end flap. Typically, this box would add about 10% to the value of the car.

In contrast, the box for the 1966 Dodge Polara below is much more interesting. In addition to an end flap stamping similar to that used for the Corvair, the box for the Dodge is colorful and features actual pictures of different 1966 Dodges on all four sides. A box of this type would add about 20% to the value of the car. Note, however, that the box and car must be in comparable condition and that the box must match the make, model, year and color of the vehicle inside.

improve. Such a promotional should have:

- no surface abrasion
- no surface rub
- no sign of repair
- no replacement parts
- no damage
- no wear
- all decals or stickers issued with the vehicle

Value Considerations

The condition criteria described previously represent the primary factors that determine the value of a plastic promotional. In addition, there are several other factors that need to be considered when determining the value as follows:

- Add 10, 15 or 20% for the original box - Some plastic promotionals were issued in colorful, attractive boxes; others, in comparatively plain boxes. The 10% addition applies to plain boxes with markings that usually only identify the contents. The 15% addition is for boxes containing moderate design and lithography such as used by Jo-Han in the late 1950's. The highest added value of 20% applies to the most colorful boxes such as those used for 1959 Pontiacs and 1969 Dodges. The same percentages apply for boxes used to ship promotionals from auto makers directly to customers. Original boxes should be in good shape and correspond to the vehicle in regard to make, model, year and color as applicable. Some mid-1950's vehicles by PMC and SMP (e.g., Chevrolets and Pontiacs) were distributed to dealerships sealed in clear cellophane or plastic and packed in a quantity of a dozen or more in a cardboard box with dividers. If still in their unopened, original wrapping, their value is increased by 25%.

- Surfaces - Surface abrasions and rubs affect eye appeal and reduce the value based on their severity. Models having chrome trim that has been partially or completely "washed off" have the same effect. Certain models such as 1960's T-Birds in dark metallic colors and similarly colored Mopars of the same era have flat or dull paint jobs. This factor is already reflected in the values listed for such vehicles.

- Windows - 10% should be added to the value of a promotional with superior windows if it is one of the models, most of 1950's vintage, that typically have window distortion problems.

Promotionals were occasionally ordered with special decals or stickers applied advertising a specific product or event. In regard to events, the vehicle maker (e.g., Ford, Chevrolet, etc.) usually had a sponsorship or support interest. The above 1971 Plymouth Barracuda has door stickers for the Rose Bowl parade.

This 1958 Cadillac Fleetwood by Jo-Han has warped (bowed) above the grill. Warpage above the grill is common for this vehicle and others of the same era and necessitates a rating of **good** as opposed to **optimal**.

■ Decals and stickers - Some promotionals, such as pace cars, derive their recognized premium values due to the decals and stickers applied. Therefore, such vehicles must have decals or stickers in a condition commensurate with their condition. For example, an optimum car should not have peeling or missing portions of decals or stickers.

■ Colors - Dealer promotionals, in part, were used to showcase new colors and color schemes. Because black was offered every year, it was not always deemed a necessary color to depict. Therefore, a black vehicle will often attract a premium value. Colors infrequently encountered and two-tone cars in dealer colors will also frequently merit a premium value largely due to their increased eye appeal. On the negative side, some colors are extremely common for certain vehicles such as metallic tan for the 1966 Buick Riviera and pale yellow for the 1962 Ford Galaxie 500. Colors as common as these for a specific car are valued less than other colors for the same car. In such cases deductions are noted in the value guide.

■ Add $5 for the original key for bank models - Some of the 1950's plastic promotionals were banks with a locked access plate on the underside. A key for access was furnished and is typically missing.

■ Advertising - The advertisements which may appear on a plastic promotional are too varied to specify an added value or percentage. To be of increased value, the advertising must have a generally universal appeal. Advertising for a local dealership or financial institution might have an added value that is limited to persons in that locale. In contrast, a vehicle with advertising promoting a product, service or event such as the Indianapolis 500 can appeal to multiple groups of collectors. Such advertising increases the demand and reduces the supply of promotionals available to collectors with the expected reflection on value.

■ Warpage - Models typically subject to warpage should be virtually straight to be considered of optimal value. As the degree of warpage increases, the value of the model decreases. Warpage on a model not typically subject to the problem reduces it to a parts vehicle status.

■ Replacement parts - Some parts for plastic promotionals can be obtained from kits or from parts manufacturers. A missing or broken part that is available and can be replaced represents a minimal value deduction of about 20%. If the replacement part is correctly installed, the car would be worth within about 10% of the listed value. If it is otherwise a top quality vehicle, it does not warrant the optimal value. If a car needs a replacement part for one that is missing or broken but such a part is not available, the value is not easily

Proper evaluation of plastic promotionals requires the application of some specific criteria depending on the make, model, year and body style. Examples of things to look for are:

Decals as applied above the rocker panels on this 1966
Ford Fairlane 500

Breaks in the sun visors, vent posts and windshield frames
on all convertibles such as this 1964 Chevrolet Impala SS

Warpage, especially on 1964 and earlier cars such as this
1959 Buick Invicta

determinable and the car should be avoided.

The condition criteria and value considerations presented above are intended to assist the collector, owner, buyer, seller, appraiser, etc. of plastic promotionals in accurately evaluating vehicles. It seems a natural human tendency to avoid reading and to rush straight to the value guide to see what an item is worth. There is also an optimistic tendency, especially on the part of owners and sellers, to overrate their item(s) and look only at the highest values provided. Impatience and optimism can result in judgement errors measured in significant dollars. This is because buyers of plastic promotionals are very condition conscious, even more so than the buyer of pot metal promotionals. The values provided in the listing that follows can be of considerable assistance. This is especially true if the user does his or her reading beforehand and properly evaluates the condition of the vehicle(s) being checked.

Repairs and repaints of plastic promotionals can be expertly rendered and difficult to detect. This 1964 Plymouth Convertible is much straighter (has less warpage) than normally encountered. The surfaces are well preserved with no adverse marks, and the color is very nice. Even the frequently broken hood ornament is intact. Nevertheless, the car would be graded as only **average** if a person notices the repair to the top of the windshield frame.

1968 AMC Javelin by Jo-Han

1968 AMC AMX by Jo-Han

1959 AMC Rambler Custom by Jo-Han

1961 AMC American by Jo-Han

1967 AMC Ambassador by Jo-Han

1975 AMC Pacer by MPC

✦✦ PLASTIC PROMOTIONALS ✦✦

YEAR	STYLE	SERIES	MAKER	NOTES	AVG.	GOOD	OPT.
▼▼▼ AEROCAR ▼▼▼							
1953	2DR		GLAD	FLYING CAR	100	200	400
▼▼▼ AMC, JAVELIN & AMX ▼▼▼							
1968	2DRHT	JAVELIN	JOH	-20% FOR FRICTION	40	75	125
1968	2DRHT	AMX	JOH	-20% FOR FRICTION	40	75	135
1969	2DRHT	JAVELIN	JOH	-20% FOR FRICTION	40	75	125
1969	2DRHT	JAVELIN	JOH	RED/WHITE/BLUE	75	125	200
1969	2DRHT	AMX	JOH	REISSUE EXISTS	40	75	135
1970	2DRHT	JAVELIN	JOH	-20% FOR FRICTION	50	75	135
1970	2DRHT	AMX	JOH	-20% FOR FRICTION	50	75	135
1971	2DRHT	JAVELIN	JOH	AMX	40	75	125
1972	2DRHT	JAVELIN	JOH	AMX, -50% FOR NON-METALLIC MEDIUM GREEN	40	75	125
▼▼▼ AMC, RAMBLER▼▼▼ (see also NASH)							
1956	4DR	CUSTOM	UNK	1/20TH, CLEAR	200	300	450
1956	4DRWGN	CUSTOM	UNK	CROSS COUNTRY	325	400	550
1959	4DRWGN	CUSTOM	JOH	-20% FOR NO INTERIOR, REISSUE EXISTS	25	50	75
1960	4DRWGN	CUSTOM	JOH	-20% FOR NO INTERIOR	25	50	75
1961	2DR	AMERICAN	JOH		50	75	125
1961	CONV.	AMERICAN	JOH		75	100	165
1961	4DRWGN	CLASSIC	JOH		25	50	75
1961	4DR	UNIT FRAME	JOH		20	30	50
1962	2DR	AMERICAN	JOH	+20 FOR DETAILED PLASTIC CHASSIS W/ FRICTION	40	60	100
1962	CONV.	AMERICAN	JOH	+20 FOR DETAILED PLASTIC CHASSIS W/ FRICTION	40	75	135
1962	4DR	CLASSIC	JOH	REISSUE EXISTS	25	50	75
1962	4DRWGN	CLASSIC	JOH		25	50	75
1963	2DR	AMERICAN	JOH		40	60	100
1963	CONV.	AMERICAN	JOH		40	75	135
1963	4DR	CLASSIC	JOH		25	50	75
1963	4DRWGN	CLASSIC	JOH		25	50	75
1964	2DRHT	AMERICAN	JOH		50	70	100
1964	CONV.	AMERICAN	JOH		75	100	150
1964	4DR	CLASSIC	JOH		50	70	100
1964	4DRWGN	CLASSIC	JOH		50	70	100
1965	2DRHT	AMERICAN	JOH	-20% FOR PALE YELLOW WITH NO FRICTION	50	70	100
1965	CONV.	AMERICAN	JOH		75	100	150
1965	4DR	CLASSIC	JOH	-20% FOR PALE YELLOW WITH NO FRICTION	50	70	100
1965	4DR	CLASSIC	JOH	TAXI	60	90	125
1965	2DRHT	MARLIN	JOH	FASTBACK	75	100	140
1965	4DRWGN	CLASSIC	JOH		50	70	100
▼▼▼ AMC, miscellaneous ▼▼▼							
1966	CONV.	AMERICAN	JOH		60	90	150
1966	2DRHT	AMBASSADOR	JOH		60	90	135
1966	2DRHT	MARLIN	JOH	FASTBACK	60	90	135
1966	4DRWGN	CLASSIC	JOH	REISSUE EXISTS	25	50	75
1967	2DRHT	AMBASSADOR	JOH	-20% FOR RADIO	30	60	115
1967	CONV.	AMBASSADOR	JOH		60	90	135
1968	2DRHT	AMBASSADOR	JOH		30	60	115
1968	CONV.	AMBASSADOR	JOH	ACTUAL CAR NEVER PRODUCED	60	90	135
1969	2DRHT	AMBASSADOR	JOH		60	80	115
1970	2DR	HORNET	JOH		15	30	60
1973	2DR	HORNET	JOH	HATCHBACK	15	30	50
1974	2DR	HORNET	JOH	HATCHBACK	15	30	50
1975	2DR	PACER	MPC	HATCHBACK	15	30	50

1955 Buick Roadmaster by AMT

1955 Buick Century by AMT

1958 Buick Roadmaster by AMT

1962 Buick Electra 225 by AMT

1955 Cadillac 62 by AMT

1966 Cadillac 62 by Jo-Han

✦✦ PLASTIC PROMOTIONALS ✦✦

▼▼▼ BUICK ▼▼▼

YEAR	STYLE	SERIES	MAKER	NOTES	AVG.	GOOD	OPT.
1954	4DR	ROADMASTER	AMT	+10% FOR WINDOWS	40	70	110
1954	CONV.	SKYLARK	AMT	-30% FOR FRICTION	90	175	325
1955	4DR	ROADMASTER	AMT	+10% FOR WINDOWS & CHROME HUBS	40	80	125
1955	CONV.	CENTURY	AMT	+10% FOR CHROME HUBS & NO FRICTION	90	150	250
1956	4DRHT	ROADMASTER	AMT	+100% WITH INTERIOR	40	60	90
1956	CONV.	CENTURY	AMT		90	175	275
1957	2DRHT	ROADMASTER	AMT	+50% WITH INTERIOR	40	60	100
1957	CONV.	ROADMASTER	AMT		60	100	165
1958	2DRHT	ROADMASTER	AMT	-30% FOR GOLD SEAT INSERTS	50	70	125
1958	CONV.	ROADMASTER	AMT	-30% FOR GOLD SEAT INSERTS	50	75	150
1959	2DRHT	INVICTA	AMT	-30% FOR 2-TONE SEATS	60	90	150
1959	CONV.	INVICTA	AMT	-30% FOR 2-TONE SEATS	60	100	165
1960	2DRHT	INVICTA	AMT	-20% FOR METAL CHASSIS	60	90	150
1960	CONV.	INVICTA	AMT	-20% FOR METAL CHASSIS	75	100	165
1960	DEMO	CHASSIS	AMT		90	200	400
1961	2DRHT	INVICTA	AMT	-20% FOR METAL CHASSIS	75	90	165
1961	4DRWGN	SPECIAL	AMT	-30% FOR FRICTION	30	60	90
1961	CONV.	INVICTA	AMT	-20% FOR METAL CHASSIS	75	100	175
1962	2DRHT	ELECTRA 225	AMT	-30% FOR FRICTION	100	185	335
1962	2DRHT	ELECTRA 225	AMT	PLATED, "A Buick Record Breaker"	100	185	335
1962	4DRWGN	SPECIAL	AMT		30	60	90
1962	CONV.	ELECTRA 225	AMT	-30% FOR FRICTION	125	225	375
1963	2DRHT	ELECTRA 225	AMT	-30% FOR FRICTION	100	165	300
1963	2DRHT	RIVIERA	AMT		100	185	335
1963	CONV.	ELECTRA 225	AMT	-30% FOR FRICTION	100	185	335
1964	2DRHT	RIVIERA	AMT		150	250	375
1964	2DRHT	WILDCAT	AMT		175	265	425
1964	CONV.	WILDCAT	AMT		175	275	425
1965	2DRHT	WILDCAT	AMT		125	250	350
1965	2DRHT	RIVIERA	AMT		90	150	225
1965	2DRHT	RIVIERA	AMT	'65 CHICAGO AUTO SHOW	90	160	240
1965	CONV.	WILDCAT	AMT		125	250	335
1966	2DRHT	RIVIERA	AMT	-50% METALLIC TAN	30	75	150
1966	2DRHT	RIVIERA	AMT	RADIO, ALL COLORS	20	35	85
1966	2DRHT	SKYLARK	AMT		100	200	325
1967	2DRHT	RIVIERA	AMT	-50% FOR FRICTION	30	75	150
1967	2DRHT	RIVIERA	AMT	RADIO	20	35	85
1968	2DRHT	RIVIERA	AMT	-20% FOR TAN	75	100	150
1969	2DRHT	WILDCAT	AMT	+10% FOR BLACK INTERIOR	50	75	125
1969	2DRHT	RIVIERA	AMT		50	75	125
1970	2DRHT	WILDCAT	AMT		50	75	125

▼▼▼ CADILLAC ▼▼▼

YEAR	STYLE	SERIES	MAKER	NOTES	AVG.	GOOD	OPT.
1955	2DRHT	62	AMT	-20% FOR NO INTERIOR	40	75	150
1956	2DRHT	62	AMT	-20% FOR NO INTERIOR	40	75	150
1958	4DRHT	FLEETWOOD	JOH	-30% FOR NO INTERIOR, REISSUE EXISTS	40	75	125
1959	4DRHT	FLEETWOOD	JOH	-30% FOR NO INTERIOR, REISSUE EXISTS	40	75	125
1960	4DRHT	FLEETWOOD	JOH	-30% FOR NO INTERIOR	40	75	125
1961	4DRHT	FLEETWOOD	JOH		55	90	150
1962	4DRHT	FLEETWOOD	JOH		65	100	175
1963	2DRHT	62	JOH		50	75	125
1963	CONV.	62	JOH		50	100	125
1964	2DRHT	62	JOH		50	100	150
1964	CONV.	62	JOH		50	100	150
1965	2DRHT	62	JOH	-20% FOR FRICTION	75	125	150
1965	CONV.	62	JOH	-20% FOR FRICTION	75	150	175
1966	2DRHT	62	JOH	-20% FOR FRICTION	100	125	150
1966	CONV.	62	JOH	-20% FOR FRICTION	75	150	175
1967	2DRHT	62	JOH	-20% FOR FRICTION	60	80	125
1967	2DRHT	ELDORADO	JOH	-20% FOR FRICTION	50	100	125

1967 Cadillac 62 by Jo-Han

1952 Chevrolet Styleline by PMC

1953 Chevrolet Bel Air by PMC

1953 Chevrolet 150 by PMC

1956 Chevrolet Bel Air by PMC

1959 Chevrolet Impala by SMP

YEAR	STYLE	SERIES	MAKER	NOTES	AVG.	GOOD	OPT.
CADILLAC, continued							
1967	CONV.	62	JOH	-20% FOR FRICTION	50	100	150
1968	2DRHT	62	JOH	-20% FOR FRICTION, REISSUE EXISTS	40	60	100
1968	2DRHT	ELDORADO	JOH	-20% FOR FRICTION	50	100	125
1968	CONV.	62	JOH	-20% FOR FRICTION, REISSUE EXISTS	30	50	100
1969	2DRHT	62	JOH	-20% FOR FRICTION	50	75	100
1969	2DRHT	ELDORADO	JOH	-20% FOR FRICTION	50	75	125
1970	2DRHT	62	JOH	-20% FOR FRICTION	30	50	125
1970	2DRHT	ELDORADO	JOH	-20% FOR FRICTION	50	75	100
1971	2DR	ELDORADO	JOH		20	40	75
1972	2DR	ELDORADO	JOH		10	30	50
1973	2DR	ELDORADO	JOH		10	20	40
1974	2DR	ELDORADO	JOH		10	15	30
1975	2DR	ELDORADO	JOH	REISSUE EXISTS	5	10	20
1976	2DR	ELDORADO	JOH	REISSUE EXISTS	5	10	20
1977	2DR	62	JOH	REISSUE EXISTS	5	10	30
1978	2DR	62	JOH	REISSUE EXISTS	5	10	30
1979	2DR	62	JOH	REISSUE EXISTS	5	10	30
▼▼▼ CHEVROLET, full-sized ▼▼▼							
1951	2DR	FLEETLINE	PMC	FASTBACK	90	125	200
1951	2DR	STYLELINE	PMC		90	125	200
1951	4DR	FLEETLINE	PMC	FASTBACK	90	150	225
1951	4DR	STYLELINE	PMC		90	125	200
1951	2DRHT	STYLELINE	PMC		100	175	235
1951	COUPE	STYLELINE	PMC		100	150	225
1951	CONV.	STYLELINE	PMC		125	225	375
1952	2DR	FLEETLINE	PMC	FASTBACK	90	125	225
1952	2DR	STYLELINE	PMC		90	125	200
1952	4DR	STYLELINE	PMC		90	125	200
1952	2DRHT	STYLELINE	PMC		100	150	235
1952	COUPE	STYLELINE	PMC		100	150	225
1952	CONV.	STYLELINE	PMC		125	225	375
1953	2DR	150	PMC		60	125	175
1953	COUPE	210	PMC		100	175	235
1953	2DR	BEL AIR	PMC		60	125	175
1953	4DR	150	PMC		60	125	175
1953	4DR	BEL AIR	PMC		60	125	175
1953	2DRHT	BEL AIR	PMC	-20% FOR BROWN	60	150	200
1953	4DRWGN	HANDYMAN	PMC	1/20TH SCALE	100	200	350
1953	CONV.	BEL AIR	PMC		125	175	325
1954	2DR	150	PMC		60	125	175
1954	2DR	210	PMC		60	150	200
1954	2DR	BEL AIR	PMC		60	125	175
1954	4DR	150	PMC		60	125	175
1954	4DR	BEL AIR	PMC	-40% FOR FRICTION	60	125	175
1954	2DRHT	BEL AIR	PMC		90	150	200
1954	CONV.	BEL AIR	PMC		125	175	225
1955	4DR	210	PMC	-20% FOR SOLID COLOR	60	125	175
1955	4DR	210	PMC	YELLOW CAB	90	150	225
1955	2DRHT	BEL AIR	PMC	-20% FOR SOLID COLOR	90	150	200
1956	4DR	BEL AIR	PMC		60	125	175
1956	4DR	BEL AIR	PMC	YELLOW CAB	90	175	250
1956	2DRHT	BEL AIR	PMC		100	150	250
1956	4DRHT	BEL AIR	PMC		90	125	200
1956	4DRWGN	BEL AIR	PMC		60	125	175
1957	2DRHT	BEL AIR	SMP	PLASTIC CHASSIS WITH NO INTERIOR	50	125	175
1957	2DRHT	BEL AIR	SMP	METAL CHASSIS W/ NO INTERIOR, -20% FOR INCORRECT HUBCAPS	20	50	75
1957	2DRHT	BEL AIR	SMP	METAL CHASSIS W/ INTERIOR, -20% FOR INCORRECT HUBCAPS	50	90	125

1961 Chevrolet Impala by SMP

1962 Chevrolet Impala SS by AMT

1963 Chevrolet Impala SS by AMT

1965 Chevrolet Impala SS by AMT

1973 Chevrolet Caprice by MPC

1968 Chevrolet Camaros by MPC

YEAR	STYLE	SERIES	MAKER	NOTES	AVG.	GOOD	OPT.

CHEVROLET, full-sized, continued

YEAR	STYLE	SERIES	MAKER	NOTES	AVG.	GOOD	OPT.
1957	4DRHT	BEL AIR	SMP		50	115	175
1957	4DRHT	BEL AIR	PMC	+10% FOR TAXI, POLICE & FIRE CHIEF VERSIONS	20	40	75
1957	4DRWGN	BEL AIR	SMP	PLASTIC CHASSIS	60	115	175
1957	4DRWGN	BEL AIR	SMP	METAL CHASSIS, - 20% FOR INCORRECT HUBCAPS	50	100	150
1957	4DRWGN	BEL AIR	PMC	+10% FOR PUBLIC SERVICE VERSIONS	20	40	75
1957	CONV.	BEL AIR	SMP	PLASTIC CHASSIS	100	175	275
1957	CONV.	BEL AIR	SMP	METAL CHASSIS, -20% FOR INCORRECT HUBCAPS	90	150	250
1958	2DRHT	IMPALA	SMP	-20% FOR NO INTERIOR	90	115	175
1958	4DRHT	BEL AIR	PMC	ALL VERSIONS WITH NO WINDOWS OR INTERIOR	30	60	90
1958	4DRHT	BEL AIR	PMC	TWO-TONE WITH WINDOWS	60	100	150
1958	4DRHT	BEL AIR	SMP	ALL VERSIONS	60	100	150
1958	4DRWGN	NOMAD	SMP	-20% FOR NO INTERIOR	60	115	150
1958	CONV.	IMPALA	SMP		60	135	200
1959	2DRHT	IMPALA	SMP	-10% FOR METAL CHASSIS	40	90	125
1959	4DR	IMPALA	PMC	ALL VERSIONS	20	60	90
1959	4DRHT	IMPALA	SMP	-10% FOR METAL CHASSIS	40	90	125
1959	4DRWGN	NOMAD	SMP	-10% FOR METAL CHASSIS	40	80	100
1959	CONV.	IMPALA	SMP	-10% FOR METAL CHASSIS	75	125	175
1960	4DR	IMPALA	PMC	ALL VERSIONS	20	50	90
1960	2DRHT	IMPALA	SMP	-10% FOR METAL CHASSIS	75	125	175
1960	4DRHT	IMPALA	SMP	-10% FOR METAL CHASSIS	40	90	125
1960	4DRWGN	NOMAD	SMP	4 TAILLIGHTS, -10% FOR METAL CHASSIS	40	90	125
1960	4DRWGN	NOMAD	SMP	6 TAILLIGHTS, -10% FOR METAL CHASSIS	40	90	125
1960	CONV.	IMPALA	SMP	-10% FOR METAL CHASSIS	75	125	175
1961	4DRHT	IMPALA	SMP	-10% FOR METAL CHASSIS	90	150	225
1961	CONV.	IMPALA	SMP	-10% FOR METAL CHASSIS	175	275	425
1962	2DRHT	IMPALA SS	AMT	+30% FOR METALLIC GOLD	165	265	375
1962	2DRHT	IMPALA SS	AMT	DELCO SHOCKS CAR, MET. BLUE, NO ENGINE	150	250	325
1962	CONV.	IMPALA SS	AMT		165	300	400
1963	2DRHT	IMPALA SS	AMT	-30% FOR FRICTION	115	185	265
1963	CONV.	IMPALA SS	AMT		135	250	350
1964	2DRHT	IMPALA SS	AMT		85	135	215
1964	CONV.	IMPALA SS	AMT	-40% FOR FRICTION	90	150	235
1965	2DRHT	IMPALA SS	AMT	-40% FOR FRICTION	75	125	200
1965	CONV.	IMPALA SS	AMT		90	150	225
1966	2DRHT	IMPALA SS	AMT	-50% FOR FRICTION	75	125	200
1966	2DRHT	IMPALA SS	AMT	RADIO	40	60	90
1966	2DRHT	IMPALA SS	AMT	BUDGET RENT-A-CAR	90	165	225
1966	CONV.	IMPALA SS	AMT		90	165	225
1967	2DRHT	IMPALA SS	AMT	-40% FOR FRICTION	85	135	185
1967	CONV.	IMPALA SS	AMT		90	165	200
1968	2DRHT	IMPALA SS	MPC	-30% FOR RADIO	85	135	185
1968	CONV.	IMPALA SS	MPC		90	165	200
1969	2DRHT	IMPALA SS	AMT		40	75	100
1969	CONV.	IMPALA SS	AMT		50	90	125
1970	2DRHT	IMPALA	AMT		40	75	100
1970	CONV.	IMPALA	AMT		50	90	125
1971	2DRHT	IMPALA	MPC		30	50	80
1971	CONV.	IMPALA	MPC		60	95	150
1972	2DRHT	IMPALA	MPC	CUSTOM	20	50	80
1973	2DRHT	CAPRICE	MPC	CLASSIC	20	50	80
1974	2DR	CAPRICE	MPC		20	30	60
1975	2DR	CAPRICE	MPC		20	30	60
1976	2DR	CAPRICE	MPC		20	30	60

▼▼▼ CHEVROLET CAMARO ▼▼▼

YEAR	STYLE	SERIES	MAKER	NOTES	AVG.	GOOD	OPT.
1967	2DRHT	SS	AMT		100	185	265
1967	CONV.	SS	AMT		125	225	315
1967	CONV.	SS	AMT	INDIANAPOLIS 500 PACE CAR	200	375	550
1967	CONV.	SS	AMT	INDIANAPOLIS 500 PACE CAR IN BUBBLE DISPLAY CASE	300	475	650

1970 Chevrolet Camaro SS by AMT

1964 Chevrolet Malibu SS by AMT

1964 Chevrolet Corvair Monza by AMT

1965 Chevrolet Corvair Corsa by AMT

1953-54 Chevrolet Corvette by PMC

1965 Chevrolet Corvette by AMT

YEAR	STYLE	SERIES	MAKER	NOTES	AVG.	GOOD	OPT.
CHEVROLET CAMARO, continued							
1968	2DRHT	SS	MPC		125	215	285
1968	CONV.	SS	MPC	+300% FOR RED	135	250	425
1969	2DRHT	SS	AMT		115	185	265
1969	CONV.	SS	AMT		135	265	335
1969	CONV.	SS	AMT	INDIANAPOLIS 500 PACE CAR	185	275	425
1970	2DR	SS	AMT	SIMULATED BLACK VINYL TOP	75	100	135
1971	2DR	SS	MPC		75	100	135
1972	2DR	SS	MPC		75	100	135
1973	2DR	SS	MPC		75	100	135
1982	2DR	Z-28	MPC		-	-	15
1983	2DR	Z-28	MPC		-	-	15
▼▼▼ CHEVROLET, CHEVELLE & MALIBU ▼▼▼							
1964	2DRHT	MALIBU SS	AMT	-30% FOR FRICTION	75	135	225
1964	4DRWGN	MALIBU	AMT		40	75	135
1965	2DRHT	MALIBU SS	AMT		150	250	350
1965	4DRWGN	MALIBU	AMT		75	100	150
1969	2DRHT	SS	AMT		75	125	185
1969	CONV.	SS	AMT	+20% FOR DARK RED	90	175	275
1970	2DRHT	SS	AMT		85	145	235
1970	CONV.	SS	AMT		90	185	285
1971	2DRHT	SS	MPC		75	115	175
1972	2DRHT	SS	MPC		75	115	175
▼▼▼ CHEVROLET CORVAIR ▼▼▼							
1960	4DR	700	SMP		50	75	125
1961	4DR	700	SMP		60	115	165
1962	2DR	MONZA	AMT		80	135	225
1963	2DR	MONZA	AMT		80	135	225
1963	CONV.	MONZA	AMT		100	165	285
1964	2DR	MONZA	AMT		85	150	250
1964	CONV.	MONZA	AMT		100	200	300
1965	2DRHT	CORSA	AMT		80	135	235
1965	CONV.	CORSA	AMT		90	165	285
1966	2DRHT	CORSA	AMT		80	125	225
1966	CONV.	CORSA	AMT		90	165	285
1967	2DRHT	MONZA	AMT		75	100	175
▼▼▼ CHEVROLET CORVETTE ▼▼▼							
1953	CONV.		PMC	WHITE, REISSUE W/ PLASTIC CHASSIS EXISTS	90	200	300
1953-54	CONV.		PMC	ALL BUT WHITE	250	400	600
1954	CONV.		PMC	SMOOTH GRAY HUBS	90	200	300
1955	CONV.		PMC	WHITE	90	200	300
1955	CONV.		PMC	ALL BUT WHITE	275	400	600
1955	CONV.		PMC	WITH '56 TAILLIGHTS	300	475	600
1958	CONV.		PMC	+50% FOR TWO-TONE WITH HARDTOP	75	125	175
1958	CONV.		SMP	-10% FOR FRICTION	75	200	400
1959	CONV.		SMP	-10% FOR FRICTION	90	200	400
1959-60	CONV.		PMC		60	125	175
1960	CONV.		SMP	-10% FOR FRICTION	90	200	400
1961	CONV.		SMP	-20% FOR FRICTION	250	450	750
1962	CONV.		AMT	-20% FOR FRICTION	250	450	750
1963	COUPE		AMT		285	375	575
1963	COUPE		PMC		60	90	175
1964	COUPE		AMT		285	375	575
1964	CONV.		AMT		285	375	575
1965	COUPE		AMT		300	400	600
1965	CONV.		AMT		300	425	625

1972 Chevrolet Corvette by MPC

1978 Chevrolet Corvette by MPC

1971 Chevrolet Monte Carlo by MPC

1958 Chevrolet Apache by SMP

1972 Chevrolet Cheyenne by MPC

1980 Chevrolet El Camino by MPC

✦✦ PLASTIC PROMOTIONALS ✦✦

YEAR	STYLE	SERIES	MAKER	NOTES	AVG.	GOOD	OPT.

CHEVROLET CORVETTE, continued

YEAR	STYLE	SERIES	MAKER	NOTES	AVG.	GOOD	OPT.
1966	COUPE		AMT		300	450	700
1966	CONV.		AMT		300	450	700
1967	COUPE		AMT		400	750	1000
1967	CONV.		AMT		400	750	1000
1968	CONV.		MPC		175	275	425
1969	COUPE		AMT		175	275	425
1969	COUPE		AMT	"TAXI CAB" YELLOW	300	600	900
1969	CONV.		AMT		175	275	425
1970	COUPE		AMT	REISSUE W/ 1970 PLATE EXISTS	165	265	400
1970	CONV.		AMT		200	325	450
1971	COUPE		MPC	USA PLATE (INTERIOR & EXTERIOR SAME COLOR)	175	275	425
1972	COUPE		MPC	+10% FOR METALLIC GOLD	165	265	385
1973	COUPE		MPC		165	265	385
1974	COUPE		MPC		150	225	325
1975	COUPE		MPC		70	100	135
1976	COUPE		MPC		70	100	135
1977	COUPE		MPC		65	90	125
1978	COUPE		MPC	WITHOUT MOLDED SIDE LINE	70	100	135
1978	COUPE		MPC	ALL BUT PREVIOUS MODEL	25	35	60
1979	COUPE		MPC		-	15	25
1980	COUPE		MPC		-	-	20
1981	COUPE		MPC	+50% FOR SILVER	-	20	35
1982	COUPE		MPC		-	20	30

▼▼▼ CHEVROLET, MONTE CARLO ▼▼▼

YEAR	STYLE	SERIES	MAKER	NOTES	AVG.	GOOD	OPT.
1970	2DRHT		AMT		80	115	165
1971	2DRHT		MPC		80	115	165
1972	2DRHT		MPC		80	115	165
1978	2DR		MPC		-	20	30
1979	2DR		MPC		10	25	35
1980	2DR		MPC		10	15	30

▼▼▼ CHEVROLET TRUCKS ▼▼▼

YEAR	STYLE	SERIES	MAKER	NOTES	AVG.	GOOD	OPT.
1956	PICKUP	CAMEO	PMC		80	115	150
1957	PICKUP	CAMEO	PMC	-50% FOR NO WINDOWS	90	135	175
1958	PICKUP	APACHE	SMP	-20% FOR CAB & BED NOT SAME COLOR	90	135	175
1958	PICKUP	CAMEO	PMC		60	90	125
1959	PICKUP	APACHE	SMP	-20% FOR 1958 REAR BUMPER	80	145	185
1959	PICKUP	APACHE	SMP	WITH 1959 REAR PAPER PLATE	85	150	180
1960	PICKUP	APACHE	SMP		60	90	150
1960	PICKUP	EL CAMINO	SMP	-10% FOR METAL CHASSIS	75	100	135
1960	PICKUP	EL CAMINO	SMP	NON-WARPING WITH '61 HUBS	80	115	145
1961	PICKUP	APACHE	SMP		90	150	235
1962	PICKUP	APACHE	AMT		90	150	235
1963	PICKUP	APACHE	AMT		90	150	235
1964	PICKUP	EL CAMINO	AMT		90	125	185
1965	PICKUP	EL CAMINO	AMT		90	125	185
1965	PICKUP	FLEETSIDE	AMT		90	150	225
1966	PICKUP	FLEETSIDE	AMT		90	150	225
1967	PICKUP	FLEETSIDE	AMT		90	125	185
1968	PICKUP	FLEETSIDE	MPC		90	125	185
1969	PICKUP	CST/10	AMT		90	125	185
1970	PICKUP	CST/10	AMT		90	125	185
1971	PICKUP	CHEYENNE	MPC		90	125	185
1972	PICKUP	CHEYENNE	MPC		90	125	185
1979	PICKUP	EL CAMINO	MPC		-	20	35
1980	PICKUP	EL CAMINO	MPC		-	20	35
1981	PICKUP	EL CAMINO	MPC		-	30	40
1982	PICKUP	EL CAMINO	MPC		-	20	35

1962 Chevrolet Chevy II by AMT

1971 Chevrolet Vega by MPC

1964 Chrysler 300 by Jo-Han

1965 Chrysler 300 by Jo-Han

1967 Chrysler 300 by Jo-Han

1960 Desoto Adventurer by Jo-Han

✦✦ PLASTIC PROMOTIONALS ✦✦

YEAR	STYLE	SERIES	MAKER	NOTES	AVG.	GOOD	OPT.
▼▼▼ CHEVROLET, miscellaneous ▼▼▼							
1962	2DRHT	CHEVY II	AMT		70	115	165
1962	CONV.	CHEVY II	AMT		90	125	200
1963	4DRWGN	CHEVY II	AMT		50	80	125
1963	CONV.	CHEVY II	AMT		90	125	200
1965	2DRHT	CHEVY II	AMT		175	300	465
1971	2DR	VEGA	MPC	HATCHBACK	-	20	50
1972	2DR	VEGA	MPC	HATCHBACK	-	20	45
1973	2DR	VEGA	MPC	HATCHBACK	-	20	45
1974	2DR	VEGA	MPC	HATCHBACK	-	20	35
1975	2DR	MONZA	MPC	HATCHBACK	-	-	25
1975	2DR	VEGA	MPC	HATCHBACK	-	-	30
1976	2DR	MONZA	MPC	HATCHBACK	-	-	25
1976	2DR	VEGA	MPC	HATCHBACK	-	-	30
1977	2DR	VEGA	MPC	HATCHBACK	-	-	30
1977	2DR	CHEVETTE	MPC	HATCHBACK	-	-	20
1977	2DR	MONZA	MPC	HATCHBACK	-	-	25
1978	2DR	CHEVETTE	MPC	HATCHBACK	-	-	20
1978	2DR	MONZA	MPC	HATCHBACK	-	-	25
1979	2DR	CHEVETTE	MPC	HATCHBACK	-	-	20
1979	2DR	MONZA	MPC	HATCHBACK	-	-	25
1980	2DR	MONZA	MPC	HATCHBACK	-	-	25
1982	2DR	CAVALIER	MPC	HATCHBACK, +20% FOR BLACK	-	-	20
1983	2DR	CAVALIER	MPC	HATCHBACK	-	-	20
▼▼▼ CHRYSLER ▼▼▼							
1957	4DRHT	NEW YORKER	JOH	+10% FOR WHITEWALLS	30	80	100
1958	4DRHT	NEW YORKER	JOH	+10% FOR WHITEWALLS	30	80	100
1959	4DRHT	NEW YORKER	JOH	+10% FOR WHITEWALLS, REISSUE EXISTS	25	80	100
1960	2DRHT	NEW YORKER	JOH	+10% FOR TORSION BARS	40	90	125
1961	2DRHT	NEW YORKER	JOH	+10% FOR TORSION BARS	50	100	135
1962	2DRHT	300	JOH	+10% FOR TORSION BARS	40	90	125
1962	CONV.	300	JOH		60	100	175
1963	2DRHT	300	JOH	+10% FOR TORSION BARS	60	100	150
1963	CONV.	300	JOH	+75% FOR INDIANAPOLIS 500 PACE CAR	60	100	175
1964	2DRHT	300	JOH	+10% FOR TORSION BARS	90	200	300
1964	2DRHT	TURBINE	JOH	BRONZE, REISSUE EXISTS	30	75	100
1964	2DRHT	TURBINE	JOH	WHITE, MOVIE CAR, REISSUE EXISTS	150	225	300
1964	CONV.	300	JOH		90	150	185
1965	2DRHT	300	JOH	+100% FOR TORSION BARS	50	90	125
1965	CONV.	300	JOH	+100% FOR TORSION BARS	75	125	165
1966	2DRHT	300	JOH	+100% FOR TORSION BARS	50	90	125
1966	CONV.	300	JOH	+100% FOR TORSION BARS	75	125	165
1967	2DRHT	300	JOH		40	60	100
1967	CONV.	300	JOH		60	90	135
1968	2DRHT	300	JOH	REISSUE EXISTS	30	50	75
1968	CONV.	300	JOH	REISSUE EXISTS	40	60	85
▼▼▼ DESOTO ▼▼▼							
1955	4DR	FIREFLITE	JOH		50	85	150
1955	4DR	FIREFLITE	IDEAL		50	85	150
1956	4DR	FIREFLITE	JOH	REISSUE EXISTS	50	85	150
1957	4DRHT	FIREFLITE	JOH	+20% FOR WHITEWALLS	40	75	100
1958	4DRHT	FIREFLITE	JOH	+20% FOR TORSION BARS	40	75	100
1959	4DRHT	FIREFLITE	JOH	+20% FOR TORSION BARS, REISSUE EXISTS	40	75	100
1960	2DRHT	ADVENTURER	JOH	+10% FOR TORSION BARS	50	80	135

1939-59 Divco Carnation van by AMT

1955 Dodge Custom Royal by AMT

1959 Dodge Custom Royal by Jo-Han

1966 Dodge Monaco 500 by MPC

1968 Dodge Coronet R/T by MPC

1970 Dodge Challenger by MPC

✦✦ PLASTIC PROMOTIONALS ✦✦

YEAR	STYLE	SERIES	MAKER	NOTES	AVG.	GOOD	OPT.
▾▾▾ DIAMOND T TRUCKS ▾▾▾							
1955	DUMP	C.O.E.	PMC	1/20TH SCALE	75	125	250
1955	SEMI	C.O.E.	PMC	1/20TH SCALE	75	125	250
▾▾▾ DIVCO TRUCKS ▾▾▾							
1939-59	DEL VAN		AMT	MADE 1950-54, REISSUE EXISTS, +20% FOR PVT. LABELS	125	275	400
1939-59	DEL VAN		AMT	DUGANS BREAD	150	325	450
1939-59	DEL VAN		AMT	CARNATION MILK	175	375	500
▾▾▾ DODGE, full-sized ▾▾▾							
1955	2DRHT	CUSTOM ROYAL	AMT	-20% WITHOUT INTERIOR	50	75	90
1955	2DRHT	CUSTOM ROYAL	AMT	TRI-COLOR WITH CHROME HUBS	90	125	150
1956	4DRHT	CUSTOM ROYAL	AMT	-30% WITHOUT INTERIOR	60	90	125
1956	4DRHT	CUSTOM ROYAL	AMT	TRI-COLOR WITH CHROME HUBS	90	125	165
1958	2DRHT	CUSTOM ROYAL	JOH	+20% FOR TORSION BARS	40	80	125
1959	2DRHT	CUSTOM ROYAL	JOH	+20% FOR TORSION BARS, REISSUE EXISTS	35	70	100
1960	2DRHT	PHOENIX	JOH	+10% FOR TORSION BARS	40	80	125
1961	2DRHT	PHOENIX	JOH	+10% FOR TORSION BARS, REISSUE EXISTS	35	70	115
1962	2DRHT	DART 440	JOH	+70% FOR GENERIC POLICE VERSION	40	65	125
1962	2DRHT	DART 440	JOH	POLICE "CAR 54 WHERE ARE YOU?"	100	150	225
1962	CONV.	DART 440	JOH		45	85	150
1963	2DRHT	POLARA	JOH	+10% FOR TORSION BARS	40	80	125
1963	CONV.	POLARA	JOH		45	85	150
1964	2DRHT	POLARA	JOH	+10% FOR TORSION BARS	50	95	165
1964	2DRHT	POLARA	JOH	50TH ANNIVERSARY MARKINGS	75	150	200
1964	CONV.	POLARA	JOH		75	115	185
1965	2DRHT	MONACO	MPC		75	150	200
1965	CONV.	CUSTOM 880	MPC		100	165	250
1966	2DRHT	MONACO 500	MPC		90	150	200
1966	2DRHT	MONACO 500	MPC	DRIVER'S TRAINING CAR	100	175	265
1966	CONV.	POLARA 500	MPC		100	175	265
1977	2DR	MONACO	MPC		-	18	25
1978	2DR	MONACO	MPC		-	18	25
▾▾▾ DODGE, mid-sized ▾▾▾							
1965	2DRHT	CORONET 500	MPC	+10% FOR DRIVER'S TRAINING CAR	200	325	525
1965	CONV.	CORONET 500	MPC		200	335	565
1968	2DRHT	CORONET R/T	MPC		100	200	285
1969	2DRHT	CORONET R/T	MPC	+10% FOR DRIVER'S TRAINING CAR	100	200	285
1969	CONV.	CORONET R/T	MPC		300	625	1500
▾▾▾ DODGE, compact ▾▾▾							
1975	2DR	DART	MPC		15	40	60
1976	2DR	DART	MPC		15	40	60
▾▾▾ DODGE CHALLENGER ▾▾▾							
1970	2DRHT		MPC	+100% FOR PLUM CRAZY COLOR	125	225	350
1971	2DRHT		MPC	+100% FOR PLUM CRAZY COLOR	125	250	375
1972	2DRHT		MPC		90	150	225
1973	2DRHT		MPC		80	100	150
▾▾▾ DODGE CHARGER ▾▾▾							
1966	2DRHT		MPC	FASTBACK	100	165	275
1967	2DRHT		MPC	FASTBACK, +10% FOR NADA 50TH ANIV. EDITION	100	185	265

1966 Dodge Charger by MPC

1971 Dodge Charger R/T by MPC

1954 Ford Crestline by AMT

1955 Ford Red Cross ambulance by PMC

1956 Ford Fairlane by AMT

1961 Ford Starliner by AMT

YEAR	STYLE	SERIES	MAKER	NOTES	AVG.	GOOD	OPT.
DODGE CHARGER, continued							
1968	2DRHT		MPC		100	185	275
1969	2DRHT	R/T	MPC		100	185	275
1970	2DRHT	R/T	MPC	+100% FOR PLUM CRAZY COLOR	100	185	275
1971	2DRHT	R/T	MPC	+50% FOR PLUM CRAZY COLOR	90	150	235
1971	2DRHT	R/T	MPC	BOBBY ALLISON #12	150	350	475
1972	2DRHT		MPC		50	100	165
1973	2DRHT		MPC		40	75	110
1974	2DRHT		MPC		40	65	90
▼▼▼ EDSEL ▼▼▼							
1958	2DRHT	PACER	AMT	TURQUOISE GREEN & WHITE	40	80	115
1958	2DRHT	PACER	AMT	OTHER COLORS, -20% FOR GOLD SIDES	100	125	225
1958	CONV.	PACER	AMT	-20% FOR GOLD SIDES	100	150	250
1959	2DRHT	CORSAIR	AMT	-20% FOR GOLD SIDES	90	125	200
1959	CONV.	CORSAIR	AMT	-20% FOR GOLD SIDES	90	150	225
1960	2DRHT	RANGER	AMT	+10% FOR PLASTIC CHASSIS	90	185	250
1960	CONV.	RANGER	AMT	+10% FOR PLASTIC CHASSIS	90	200	265
▼▼▼ FORD, full-sized ▼▼▼							
1949	4DR	CUSTOM	AMT	ALL VERSIONS	50	75	125
1950	4DR	CUSTOM	AMT		50	80	135
1950	4DR	CUSTOM	AMT	UNASSEMBLED IN BOY SCOUT BOX	100	175	225
1951	4DR	CUSTOM	AMT	ALL VERSIONS	50	80	135
1952	4DR	CUSTOMLINE	AMT	-10% FOR NO WINDOWS	40	75	125
1953	4DR	CUSTOMLINE	AMT	-10% FOR NO WINDOWS	40	75	125
1953	CONV.	CRESTLINE	AMT		50	100	150
1953	CONV.	CRESTLINE	AMT	INDIANAPOLIS 500 PACE CAR, SPARE HAS HUBCAP ON FACTORY PROMOTIONAL	100	250	350
1953	CONV.	CRESTLINE	AMT	INDIANAPOLIS 500 PACE CAR KIT, UNBUILT & COMPLETE WITH DECALS IN ORIGINAL BOX	-	-	750
1954	4DR	CUSTOMLINE	AMT	-10% FOR NO WINDOWS	40	75	125
1954	CONV.	CRESTLINE	AMT		75	125	200
1955	2DRHT	FAIRLANE	AMT	+20% FOR CHROME HUBS & WINDOWS	40	60	100
1955	2DRHT	FAIRLANE	AMT	WITH INTERIOR	65	80	135
1955	4DRWGN	COUNTRY SEDAN	PMC	+10% FOR RED CROSS	90	150	200
1955	CONV.	FAIRLANE	AMT	+10% FOR CHROME HUBS	90	150	200
1956	4DRHT	FAIRLANE	AMT	-30% FOR NO INTERIOR	75	100	150
1956	4DRWGN	COUNTRY SEDAN	PMC	+10% FOR RED CROSS	90	150	200
1956	CONV.	FAIRLANE	AMT		100	185	225
1957	2DR	CUSTOM 300	AMT	-10% FOR INCORRECT HUBCAPS	100	250	350
1957	2DRHT	FAIRLANE 500	AMT	-30% FOR NO INTERIOR	40	80	125
1957	4DRWGN	COUNTRY SEDAN	PMC	-20% FOR SOLID COLOR & NO WINDOWS	60	90	125
1957	CONV.	FAIRLANE 500	AMT		75	125	185
1958	2DRHT	FAIRLANE 500	AMT		75	100	145
1958	4DRWGN	COUNTRY SEDAN	PMC	-20% FOR SOLID COLOR & NO WINDOWS	50	90	125
1958	CONV.	FAIRLANE 500	AMT		70	115	165
1959	2DRHT	FAIRLANE 500	AMT		90	125	150
1959	2DRHT	GALAXIE	AMT		75	100	125
1959	4DRWGN	COUNTRY SEDAN	PMC	-40% FOR NO INTERIOR	75	100	125
1959	4DRWGN	COUNTRY SEDAN	PMC	"FORD AIRE" ON REAR TAIL GATE	85	110	150
1959	CONV.	FAIRLANE 500	AMT		90	135	175
1959	CONV.	GALAXIE	AMT		85	125	165
1960	4DR	FAIRLANE	HUB	1/24TH, -50% FOR NO WINDOWS & NO INTERIOR	60	100	125
1960	2DRHT	STARLINER	AMT	+20% FOR PLASTIC CHASSIS	40	65	115
1960	4DRHT	GALAXIE	AMT	+20% FOR PLASTIC CHASSIS	40	60	90
1960	4DRWGN	COUNTRY SEDAN	HUB	1/24TH, -20% FOR SOLID LIGHT BLUE	60	90	125
1960	CONV.	GALAXIE	AMT	+10% FOR PLASTIC CHASSIS	75	100	135
1961	4DR	FAIRLANE	HUB	1/24TH	60	90	125
1961	2DRHT	GALAXIE	AMT	ALL VERSIONS, +20% FOR PLASTIC CHASSIS	40	65	115

1962 Ford Galaxie 500 by AMT

1966 Ford Galaxie 500 by AMT

1969 Ford Torino by AMT

1963 Ford Falcon by AMT

1970-71 Ford Maverick by Jo-Han

1965 Ford Mustang by AMT

YEAR	STYLE	SERIES	MAKER	NOTES	AVG.	GOOD	OPT.

FORD, full-sized, continued

YEAR	STYLE	SERIES	MAKER	NOTES	AVG.	GOOD	OPT.
1961	2DRHT	STARLINER	AMT	ALL VERSIONS, +20% FOR PLASTIC CHASSIS	75	125	165
1961	4DRWGN	COUNTRY SEDAN	HUB	ALL VERSIONS, 1/24TH, -20% FOR LIGHT GREEN	60	90	125
1961	CONV.	GALAXIE	AMT	+20% FOR PLASTIC CHASSIS	60	90	135
1962	2DRHT	GALAXIE 500	AMT	-20% FOR FRICTION OR PALE YELLOW	60	90	125
1962	CONV.	GALAXIE 500	AMT	-20% FOR FRICTION	75	125	165
1962	CONV.	GALAXIE 500	AMT	LIGHT BLUE W/ TOP UP	125	250	350
1962	4DRWGN	COUNTRY SEDAN	HUB	1/24TH, -20% FOR BEIGE	60	90	125
1963	2DRHT	GALAXIE 500	AMT	-20% FOR FRICTION	50	90	125
1963	CONV.	GALAXIE 500	AMT	-20% FOR FRICTION, -20% FOR BEIGE	75	125	175
1964	2DRHT	GALAXIE 500	AMT	-20% FOR FRICTION, BLACK RESISSUE EXISTS	65	90	150
1964	CONV.	GALAXIE 500	AMT	-20% FOR FRICTION	75	125	175
1965	2DRHT	GALAXIE 500	AMT	-20% FOR FRICTION	60	90	125
1965	CONV.	GALAXIE 500	AMT	-20% FOR FRICTION	80	115	165
1966	2DRHT	GALAXIE 500	AMT	-20% FOR FRICTION	60	90	125
1966	CONV.	GALAXIE 500	AMT		75	125	175
1967	2DRHT	GALAXIE 500	AMT		60	90	125
1968	2DRHT	GALAXIE 500	AMT		45	70	100
1969	2DRHT	GALAXIE 500XL	AMT		45	70	100
1970	4DRHT	LTD	AMT		45	70	100

▼▼▼ FORD, mid-sized ▼▼▼

YEAR	STYLE	SERIES	MAKER	NOTES	AVG.	GOOD	OPT.
1962	2DR	FAIRLANE 500	AMT	-20% FOR METALLIC TURQUOISE	40	80	135
1963	2DRHT	FAIRLANE 500	AMT	ALL VERSIONS	60	90	125
1964	2DRHT	FAIRLANE 500	AMT	-20% FOR FRICTION	50	90	125
1965	2DRHT	FAIRLANE 500	AMT		50	90	125
1966	2DRHT	FAIRLANE 500	AMT	BLACK OR WHITE RETSSUES W/ MAROON INT. EXIST	75	125	175
1969	2DRHT	TORINO	AMT	-10% FOR BLUE	75	125	175
1970	2DRHT	TORINO	AMT	COBRA, "FAIRLANE" ON BOX	75	150	225
1971	2DRHT	TORINO	AMT	COBRA	75	175	250
1972	2DRHT	GRAN TORINO	JOH	BUTTERSCOTCH OR BLUE	20	35	60

▼▼▼ FORD, compact ▼▼▼

YEAR	STYLE	SERIES	MAKER	NOTES	AVG.	GOOD	OPT.
1960	2DR	FALCON	AMT	ALL VERSIONS	15	30	60
1961	2DR	FALCON	AMT	ALL VERSIONS, -20% FOR FRICTION	30	75	95
1962	2DR	FALCON	AMT	FUTURA	40	75	100
1963	CONV.	FALCON	AMT	FUTURA	75	135	185
1964	2DRHT	FALCON	AMT	SPRINT, -20% FOR RED	65	125	175
1964	CONV.	FALCON	AMT	SPRINT	75	135	185
1965	2DRHT	FALCON	AMT	SPRINT	65	125	175
1965	CONV.	FALCON	AMT	SPRINT	75	135	185
1966	2DR	FALCON	AMT	FUTURA	50	90	125
1970-71	2DR	MAVERICK	JOH		15	35	60

▼▼▼ FORD MUSTANG ▼▼▼

YEAR	STYLE	SERIES	MAKER	NOTES	AVG.	GOOD	OPT.
1965	2DRHT		AMT	ALSO CALLED A 1964½ MODEL	60	100	150
1965	2DRHT		AMT	INDIANAPOLIS 500 PACE CAR, INDY 1964	90	175	225
1965	2DR		AMT	FASTBACK, +40% FOR WHITE	90	125	175
1966	2DRHT		AMT	-20% FOR FRICTION	90	125	150
1966	2DRHT		AMF	LARGE SCALE W/ ELECTRIC MOTOR	75	125	200
1966	2DR		AMT	FASTBACK, -50% FOR RADIO	150	250	375
1967	2DR		AMT	FASTBACK, -30% FOR YELLOW, -50% FOR RADIO	150	250	325
1967	2DR		AMF	FASTBACK, LARGE SCALE W/ ELECTRIC MOTOR	75	125	200
1967	2DR		AMF	FASTBACK, LARGE SCALE W/ GAS MOTOR	85	150	250
1969	2DRHT	MACH I	AMT	FASTBACK	450	675	1000
1971	2DRHT	MACH I	AMT	FASTBACK	90	175	250
1972	2DRHT	MACH I	AMT	FASTBACK	90	175	250
1974	2DR	MUSTANG II	MPC	HATCHBACK	15	30	50

1975 Ford Mustang Mach II by MPC

1971 Ford Pinto by Eldon

1971-72 Ford Pinto by AMT

1962 Ford Thunderbird by AMT

1963 Ford Thunderbird by AMT

1961 Ford Ranchero by AMT

YEAR	STYLE	SERIES	MAKER	NOTES	AVG.	GOOD	OPT.
FORD MUSTANG, continued							
1975	2DR	MACH II	MPC	HATCHBACK	15	30	50
1981	2DR	COBRA	UMC	HATCHBACK	-	15	25
▼▼▼ FORD PINTO ▼▼▼							
1971	2DR		ELDON	ELECTRIC MOTOR, +50% FOR UNASSEMBELED IN BOX	-	20	40
1972	2DR		AMT	HATCHBACK	-	20	40
▼▼▼ FORD THUNDERBIRD ▼▼▼							
1955	CONV.		AMT		75	135	225
1956	CONV.		AMT		85	150	250
1957	CONV.		AMT	-60% FOR RED	75	135	225
1958	2DRHT		AMT	-20% FOR GOLD SEAT INSERTS	50	90	125
1959	2DRHT		AMT		50	90	125
1959	CONV.		AMT		60	95	150
1960	2DRHT		AMT	-20% FOR METAL CHASSIS	50	90	125
1960	CONV.		AMT	-20% FOR METAL CHASSIS	60	95	150
1961	2DRHT		AMT	BEIGE, -20% FOR METAL CHASSIS	40	75	100
1961	2DRHT		AMT	ALL BUT BEIGE, -20% FOR METAL CHASSIS	50	90	125
1961	CONV.		AMT	-20% FOR METAL CHASSIS	80	115	165
1962	2DRHT		AMT	-20% FOR FRICTION, -20% FOR WHITE	50	90	125
1962	CONV.		AMT	-20% FOR FRICTION, -20% FOR WHITE	90	165	250
1962	CONV.		AMT	NO SKIRTS, -20% FOR FRICTION, -20% FOR WHITE	100	175	275
1962	CONV.	SPORTS RDSTR	AMT	-20% FOR FRICTION	150	250	350
1963	2DRHT		AMT	-20% FOR FRICTION, +30% FOR SKIRTS -20% FOR ROSE-BEIGE METALLIC	65	115	150
1963	CONV.		AMT	-20% FOR FRICTION, +30% FOR SKIRTS -25% FOR WHITE	90	165	235
1963	CONV.	SPORTS RDSTR	AMT	-20% FOR FRICTION	175	275	375
1964	2DRHT		AMT	-50% FOR RADIO	50	90	125
1964	CONV.		AMT		80	135	200
1965	2DRHT		AMT	-50% FOR RADIO	50	90	125
1965	CONV.		AMT	-20% FOR FRICTION	70	115	185
1966	2DRHT		AMT	-50% FOR RADIO, -20% FOR FRICTION	50	90	125
1967	2DRHT		AMT	-30% FOR RADIO, -10% FOR FRICTION	25	40	75
1968	2DRHT		AMT	-30% FOR RADIO, -10% FOR FRICTION	25	40	75
1969	2DRHT		AMT	-20% FOR RADIO	50	75	100
1970	2DRHT		AMT		50	75	100
1971	2DRHT		AMT		50	75	100
▼▼▼ FORD TRUCKS ▼▼▼							
1959	PICKUP	RANCHERO	PMC	-40% FOR NO INTERIOR	50	90	125
1960	PICKUP	F-100	AMT		90	150	225
1961	PICKUP	RANCHERO	AMT	FALCON	75	100	135
1961	PICKUP	F-100	AMT		90	150	225
1962	PICKUP	F-100	AMT		100	185	275
1963	PICKUP	F-100	AMT		100	185	275
1963	PICKUP	F-100	AMT	PLATED WITH 64-66 PLATES	60	100	125
▼▼▼ GREYHOUND BUS ▼▼▼							
1958	BUS		BELL	GMC	100	225	350
▼▼▼ HUDSON ▼▼▼							
1948-49	4DR	COMMODORE	HUD	12.5", CLEAR BODY BOTH FULLY & HALF PAINTED	275	450	775

1963 Imperial Crown by AMT

1965 Imperial Crown by AMT

1947-49 International KB-1 by PMC

1949-58 International Metro by PMC

1953-55 International R-110 Dri-gas by PMC

1951 Kaiser Henry J by Banthrico

◆◆ PLASTIC PROMOTIONALS ◆◆

YEAR	STYLE	SERIES	MAKER	NOTES	AVG.	GOOD	OPT.
▼▼▼ IMPERIAL ▼▼▼							
1958	2DRHT	CROWN	SMP	+10% FOR SOLID COLOR	50	90	125
1958	CONV.	CROWN	SMP		50	90	125
1959	2DRHT	CROWN	SMP	SPARE APPLIED OR INCLUDED IN MOLD	50	90	125
1959	CONV.	CROWN	SMP	SPARE APPLIED OR INCLUDED IN MOLD	50	90	125
1960	2DRHT	CROWN	SMP	+20% FOR PLASTIC CHASSIS	50	90	125
1960	CONV.	CROWN	SMP	+20% FOR PLASTIC CHASSIS	50	90	125
1961	2DRHT	CROWN	AMT	ALL VERSIONS	115	200	375
1961	CONV.	CROWN	AMT	ALL VERSIONS	115	200	375
1962	2DRHT	CROWN	AMT		100	200	325
1962	CONV.	CROWN	AMT		150	335	500
1963	2DRHT	CROWN	AMT		125	225	350
1963	CONV.	CROWN	AMT		125	250	400
1964	2DRHT	CROWN	AMT		125	265	425
1964	CONV.	CROWN	AMT		125	275	435
1965	2DRHT	CROWN	AMT		150	265	425
1965	CONV.	CROWN	AMT		150	275	435
1966	2DRHT	CROWN	AMT		150	265	425
1966	CONV.	CROWN	AMT		150	275	435
1967	2DRHT	CROWN	JOH		65	100	150
1968	2DRHT	CROWN	JOH	REISSUE EXISTS	30	50	90
▼▼▼ INTERNATIONAL TRUCKS ▼▼▼							
1947-49	PICKUP	KB-1	PMC		90	185	275
1949-58	DEL VAN	METRO	PMC	DOUBLE REAR DOOR MOLDED AS ONE	75	100	150
1949-58	DEL VAN	METRO	PMC	OLIVE WITH U.S. MAIL MARKINGS	150	275	450
1950-52	PICKUP	L-110	PMC		100	225	350
1950-52	DUMP	L	PMC		100	275	450
1950-52	STAKE	L	PMC		100	275	450
1950-52	SEMI	L	PMC	+10% FOR MAYFLOWER	100	275	450
1953-55	PICKUP	R-110	PMC		100	225	350
1953-55	PICKUP	R-110	PMC	DRI-GAS, YELLOW W/ 15 GREEN PROPANE TANKS	125	275	450
1953-55	DUMP	R	PMC		100	275	450
1953-55	STAKE	R	PMC		100	275	450
1953-55	SEMI	R	PMC	+10% FOR MAYFLOWER	100	275	450
1955-59	SEMI	C.O.E.	PMC	1/20TH SCALE	50	90	125
1955-59	DUMP	C.O.E.	PMC	1/20TH SCALE	50	90	125
1956-57	PICKUP	S-110	PMC	REISSUE EXISTS	100	200	300
1956-57	DUMP	S	PMC		100	250	450
1956-57	STAKE	S	PMC		100	250	450
1956-57	SEMI	S	PMC	+10% FOR MAYFLOWER	125	275	450
1957	PICKUP	A-100	PMC	GOLD & WHITE ANNIVERSARY, +40% FOR COASTER	40	75	125
1957	PICKUP	A-100	PMC	2-TONE COLORS OTHER THAN GOLD & WHITE	90	135	200
1957	PICKUP	A-100	PMC	SOLID COLOR, NO WINDOWS, WARPING PLASTIC	25	50	75
1957	STAKE	A	PMC	WARPING PLASTIC	75	100	175
1957	SEMI	A	PMC	WARPING PLASTIC	90	150	275
1957	DUMP	A	PMC	WARPING PLASTIC	75	100	175
1958	PICKUP	A-100	PMC	SOLID COLOR, NO WINDOWS, NON-WARPING PLASTIC	25	50	100
1958	STAKE	A	PMC	NON-WARPING PLASTIC	75	125	200
1958	SEMI	A	PMC	NON-WARPING PLASTIC	100	150	225
1958	DUMP	A	PMC	NON-WARPING PLASTIC	75	125	200
1959	DEL VAN	METRO	PMC	SINGLE REAR DOOR	50	75	100
▼▼▼ KAISER ▼▼▼							
1949-50	4DRCONV	DELUXE	TF	11 3/4" WITH KEY WIND	100	200	325
1951	2DR	HENRY J	BAN	WITH WINDOWS & HUBCAPS	125	175	265
1951	2DR	HENRY J	LINC	WITHOUT WINDOWS & HUBCAPS	90	125	175
1951	2DR	HENRY J	LINC	RACE CAR VERSION	125	175	325
1951	2DR	HENRY J	IDEAL	2-INCH, SINGLE PIECE	15	45	75

1966 Continental by AMT

1958-63 Mercedes-Benz 300SL by Hubley

1961 Mercury Monterey by AMT

1966 Mercury Park Lane by AMT

1963 Mercury Comet S-22 by AMT

1962 Mercury Meteor Custom by AMT

✦✦ PLASTIC PROMOTIONALS ✦✦

YEAR	STYLE	SERIES	MAKER	NOTES	AVG.	GOOD	OPT.
KAISER, continued							
1951	4DR	MANHATTAN	IDEAL	2-INCH, SINGLE PIECE	15	45	75

▾▾▾ LINCOLN & CONTINENTAL ▾▾▾

YEAR	STYLE	SERIES	MAKER	NOTES	AVG.	GOOD	OPT.
1956	2DRHT	MARK II	AMT	3 SCREWS, -50% FOR NO INTERIOR	75	100	150
1957	2DRHT	MARK II	AMT	4 SCREWS, -50% FOR NO INTERIOR	90	125	175
1958	4DRHT	MARK III	AMT	+20% FOR WHITE SEAT INSERTS	40	85	125
1959	2DRHT	MARK IV	AMT		40	85	125
1959	CONV.	MARK IV	AMT		40	85	125
1960	2DRHT	MARK V	AMT	+40% FOR PLASTIC CHASSIS	40	85	125
1960	CONV.	MARK V	AMT	+40% FOR PLASTIC CHASSIS	40	90	135
1961	4DR		AMT	+20% FOR PLASTIC CHASSIS	80	125	175
1961	4DRCONV		AMT	+20% FOR PLASTIC CHASSIS	100	200	325
1962	4DR		AMT		90	150	250
1962	4DRCONV		AMT		175	300	400
1963	4DR		AMT		125	175	300
1963	4DRCONV		AMT		200	350	425
1964	4DR		AMT		125	175	300
1965	4DR		AMT		75	100	150
1966	4DR		AMT		75	100	150
1967	4DR		AMT		70	90	125
1968	4DR		AMT		50	75	100

▾▾▾ MERCEDES-BENZ ▾▾▾

YEAR	STYLE	SERIES	MAKER	NOTES	AVG.	GOOD	OPT.
1958-63	2DR	300SL	HUB	1/24TH, -50% FOR NO WINDOWS & NO INTERIOR	40	75	125
1958-63	CONV.	300SL	HUB	1/24TH, -50% FOR NO WINDOWS & NO INTERIOR	40	75	125

▾▾▾ MERCURY ▾▾▾

YEAR	STYLE	SERIES	MAKER	NOTES	AVG.	GOOD	OPT.
1959	2DRHT	PARK LANE	AMT	+20% FOR SOLID COLOR SEATS	35	60	100
1959	CONV.	PARK LANE	AMT	+20% FOR SOLID COLOR SEATS	40	70	150
1960	2DRHT	PARK LANE	AMT	+20% FOR PLASTIC CHASSIS	40	75	125
1960	CONV.	PARK LANE	AMT	+20% FOR PLASTIC CHASSIS	50	85	165
1961	2DRHT	MONTEREY	AMT	-20% FOR METAL CHASSIS	40	75	125
1961	CONV.	MONTEREY	AMT	-20% FOR METAL CHASSIS	75	125	185
1962	2DRHT	MONTEREY	AMT		90	150	225
1962	CONV.	MONTEREY	AMT		100	165	250
1963	CONV.	MONTEREY	AMT		200	300	450
1964	2DRHT	PARK LANE	AMT	BREEZEWAY WINDOW	165	250	385
1965	2DRHT	PARK LANE	AMT	-20% FOR FRICTION	50	90	125
1966	2DRHT	PARK LANE	AMT	-20% FOR FRICTION	50	90	125

▾▾▾ MERCURY COMET ▾▾▾

YEAR	STYLE	SERIES	MAKER	NOTES	AVG.	GOOD	OPT.
1960	2DR	DELUXE	AMT		20	45	85
1960	4DR	DELUXE	AMT		20	45	75
1961	2DR	CUSTOM	AMT	-20% FOR FRICTION	25	50	90
1962	2DR	CUSTOM	AMT	-20% FOR FRICTION	35	60	100
1963	CONV.	S-22	AMT		165	225	375
1964	2DRHT	CALIENTE	AMT		165	225	375
1966	2DRHT	CYCLONE	AMT		75	115	150
1966	2DRHT	CYCLONE	AMT	INDIANAPOLIS 500 PACE CAR, RED OR WHITE	100	200	300
1971-72	2DR		JOH		10	25	45

▾▾▾ MERCURY METEOR ▾▾▾

YEAR	STYLE	SERIES	MAKER	NOTES	AVG.	GOOD	OPT.
1962	2DR	CUSTOM	AMT		100	200	300
1963	2DRHT	S-33	AMT		125	250	325

1949 Oldsmobile 98 by Cruver

1958 Oldsmobile 98 by Jo-Han

1963 Oldsmobile Starfire by Jo-Han

1966 Oldsmobile Toronado by Jo-Han

1962 Oldsmobile F-85 by Jo-Han

1968 Oldsmobile 4-4-2 by Jo-Han

✦✦ PLASTIC PROMOTIONALS ✦✦

YEAR	STYLE	SERIES	MAKER	NOTES	AVG.	GOOD	OPT.

▼▼▼ METROPOLITAN (Nash) ▼▼▼

YEAR	STYLE	SERIES	MAKER	NOTES	AVG.	GOOD	OPT.
1959-62	2DR	1500	HUB	1/24TH, -60% FOR NO WINDOWS & NO INTERIOR	150	225	300
1959-62	CONV.	1500	HUB	1/24TH, -60% FOR NO WINDOWS & NO INTERIOR	150	225	300

▼▼▼ NASH ▼▼▼ (see AMC for RAMBLER after 1954)

YEAR	STYLE	SERIES	MAKER	NOTES	AVG.	GOOD	OPT.
1952	4DR	AMBASSADOR	PMC		50	90	150
1953	4DR	AMBASSADOR	PMC	+20% FOR 2-TONE	50	90	150
1954	4DR	AMBASSADOR	PMC		75	125	175

▼▼▼ OLDSMOBILE, full-sized ▼▼▼

YEAR	STYLE	SERIES	MAKER	NOTES	AVG.	GOOD	OPT.
1949	4DR	98	CRU	1/25.5TH SCALE, +50% FOR RED, RESIN REISSUE EXISTS	175	275	350
1956	4DRHT	98	JOH	-30% FOR NO INTERIOR, REISSUE EXISTS	50	90	150
1957	4DRHT	98	JOH	-30% FOR NO INTERIOR, REISSUE EXISTS	40	85	125
1958	4DRHT	98	JOH	-30% FOR NO INTERIOR, REISSUE EXISTS	40	85	125
1959	4DRHT	98	JOH	-30% FOR NO INTERIOR	40	85	125
1959	4DRHT	98	JOH	WITH DETAILED CHASSIS	50	90	135
1960	2DRHT	98	JOH	+10% FOR DETAILED CHASSIS	50	85	125
1961	4DRHT	88	JOH	+10% FOR DETAILED CHASSIS	50	100	135
1962	4DRHT	88	JOH	+10% FOR DETAILED CHASSIS	50	100	135
1963	2DRHT	STARFIRE	JOH	+10% FOR DETAILED CHASSIS, REISSUE EXISTS	25	50	75
1963	CONV.	STARFIRE	JOH	+10% FOR DETAILED CHASSIS, REISSUE EXISTS	30	60	85
1965	2DRHT	88	AMT	-50% FOR RADIO	75	115	150
1965	CONV.	88	AMT		90	135	175
1966	2DRHT	TORONADO	JOH	-20% FOR FRICTION	40	75	100
1967	2DRHT	TORONADO	JOH	WITH '66 HUBCAPS & FRICTION	25	50	75
1967	2DRHT	TORONADO	MPC	WITH '67 HUBCAPS & DETAILED CHASSIS	40	75	100
1968	2DRHT	TORONADO	JOH	-20% FOR FRICTION	25	50	75
1969	2DRHT	TORONADO	JOH	-20% FOR FRICTION	25	50	75
1970	2DRHT	TORONADO	JOH		25	50	75
1971	2DRHT	TORONADO	JOH		25	50	80
1972	2DRHT	TORONADO	JOH	+20% FOR 75TH ANNIVERSARY	25	50	80

▼▼▼ OLDSMOBILE F-85 & CUTLASS ▼▼▼

YEAR	STYLE	SERIES	MAKER	NOTES	AVG.	GOOD	OPT.
1961	4DRWGN	DELUXE	JOH	F-85	15	40	80
1962	2DR		JOH	F-85, REISSUE EXISTS	15	40	80
1962	CONV.		JOH	F-85	35	50	100
1964	2DRHT		JOH	+10% FOR 1964 CHICAGO AUTO SHOW	70	115	175
1964	CONV.		JOH		90	125	185
1968	2DRHT	4-4-2	JOH	-20% FOR FRICTION	60	90	135
1969	2DRHT	4-4-2	JOH	-20% FOR FRICTION	60	90	135
1970	2DRHT	4-4-2	JOH	REISSUE EXISTS	40	75	100
1971	2DRHT	4-4-2	JOH		60	90	135
1973	2DR		JOH		-	25	50
1974	2DR		JOH		-	20	40
1975	2DR		JOH	REISSUE EXISTS	-	15	30

▼▼▼ OPEL ▼▼▼

YEAR	STYLE	SERIES	MAKER	NOTES	AVG.	GOOD	OPT.
1959-60	2DR	REKORD	PMC	-30% FOR NO WINDOWS OR INTERIOR	20	50	75
1969	COUPE	GT	AMT	RED	75	135	175
1970	COUPE	GT	AMT	MET. GREEN	75	135	175

▼▼▼ PACKARD ▼▼▼

YEAR	STYLE	SERIES	MAKER	NOTES	AVG.	GOOD	OPT.
1951	AMB		AMT	1/20TH, HENNEY AMBULANCE, ALL VERSIONS	200	450	775

1950 Plymouth Special Deluxe by PMC

1959 Plymouth Fury by Jo-Han

1962 Plymouth Fury by Jo-Han

1964 Plymouth Fury by Jo-Han

1966 Plymouth Fury III by Jo-Han

1968 Plymouth Fury III by Jo-Han

YEAR	STYLE	SERIES	MAKER	NOTES	AVG.	GOOD	OPT.
▼▼▼ **PLYMOUTH, full-sized** ▼▼▼							
1949	4DR	SPEC. DELUXE	AMT		40	90	150
1950	4DR	SPEC. DELUXE	AMT	ALL VERSIONS	35	85	125
1950	2DRWGN	SPEC. DELUXE	PMC	1/20TH	90	200	300
1951	4DR	CRANBROOK	PMC	1/20TH	150	275	400
1951	2DRWGN	SPEC. DELUXE	PMC	1/20TH	90	200	300
1952	4DR	CRANBROOK	PMC	1/20TH	150	275	400
1952	2DRWGN	CONCORD	PMC	1/20TH, ALL VERSIONS	90	200	300
1953	4DR	CRANBROOK	PMC		25	50	100
1954	4DR	BELVEDERE	PMC	-30% FOR NO WINDOWS	30	50	125
1954	4DR	BELVEDERE	PMC	POLICE & FIRE, +20% FOR BLACK POLICE	40	60	90
1954	2DRWGN	BELVEDERE	PMC	-30% FOR NO WINDOWS	40	90	125
1954	2DRWGN	BELVEDERE	PMC	AMBULANCE, -30% FOR NO WINDOWS	40	90	125
1954	4DR	BELVEDERE	PMC	TAXI, YELLOW, -30% FOR NO WINDOWS	40	100	175
1954	4DR	BELVEDERE	PMC	TAXI, RED, "LeCLEDE"	150	300	400
1955	4DR	BELVEDERE	JOH	-10% FOR FRICTION	75	100	150
1955	4DR	BELVEDERE	JOH	TAXI	90	150	200
1955	4DR	BELVEDERE	IDEAL		75	100	150
1956	4DR	BELVEDERE	JOH	-10% FOR FRICTION, REISSUE EXISTS	40	90	125
1956	4DR	BELVEDERE	JOH	TAXI, REISSUE EXISTS	50	95	150
1957	2DRHT	BELVEDERE	JOH	TAXI	80	125	175
1957	2DRHT	BELVEDERE	JOH	-20% FOR REAR NOT 2-TONE	50	90	125
1957	2DRHT	BELVEDERE	JOH	"SEASONS GREETINGS FROM RAY ANTHONY"	60	100	150
1958	2DRHT	BELVEDERE	JOH	-20% FOR FRICTION	50	90	125
1958	2DRHT	FURY	JOH		60	125	200
1958	2DRHT	BELVEDERE	JOH	TAXI	80	125	175
1959	2DRHT	FURY	JOH	-20% FOR FRICTION, REISSUE EXISTS	50	75	100
1959	2DRHT	FURY	JOH	TAXI	80	125	175
1960	2DRHT	FURY	JOH	+20% FOR TORSION BARS	50	75	100
1960	2DRHT	FURY	JOH	TAXI	80	125	175
1960	4DRWGN	SPORT SUBURB.	JOH	+20% FOR TORSION BARS	40	60	90
1961	2DRHT	FURY	JOH	+20% FOR TORSION BARS	40	60	100
1961	2DRHT	FURY	JOH	TAXI OR POLICE CAR	100	150	200
1962	2DRHT	FURY	JOH	+20% FOR TORSION BARS	40	60	125
1962	CONV.	FURY	JOH	+20% FOR TORSION BARS	40	65	150
1962	2DRHT	FURY	JOH	TAXI OR POLICE CAR	85	135	200
1963	2DRHT	FURY	JOH	+20% FOR TORSION BARS	40	60	100
1963	CONV.	FURY	JOH	+20% FOR TORSION BARS	40	65	150
1964	2DRHT	FURY	JOH	+20% FOR TORSION BARS	80	115	175
1964	CONV.	FURY	JOH	+20% FOR TORSION BARS	90	135	225
1965	2DRHT	FURY III	JOH	+20% FOR TORSION BARS	75	100	150
1965	CONV.	FURY III	JOH	+20% FOR TORSION BARS	90	115	185
1965	CONV.	FURY III	JOH	INDIANAPOLIS 500 PACE CAR	175	200	300
1965	2DRHT	FURY III	JOH	DRIVER'S TRAINING CAR	90	100	150
1966	2DRHT	FURY III	JOH	+20% FOR TORSION BARS	75	100	165
1966	2DRHT	FURY III	JOH	DRIVER'S TRAINING CAR	90	125	200
1966	CONV.	FURY III	JOH	+20% FOR TORSION BARS	85	125	200
1967	2DRHT	FURY III	JOH	-20% FOR FRICTION	40	75	100
1967	2DRHT	FURY III	JOH	DRIVER'S TRAINING CAR	90	125	175
1967	CONV.	FURY III	JOH	-20% FOR FRICTION	60	100	125
1968	2DRHT	FURY III	JOH	-20% FOR FRICTION	40	75	100
1968	2DRHT	FURY III	JOH	DRIVER'S TRAINING CAR	90	125	175
1968	CONV.	FURY III	JOH	-20% FOR FRICTION	60	100	125
▼▼▼ **PLYMOUTH, mid-sized** ▼▼▼							
1969	2DRHT	GTX	JOH	-20% FOR FRICTION	60	90	135
1969	2DRHT	GTX	JOH	DRIVER'S TRAINING CAR	100	165	200
1970	2DRHT	GTX	JOH	-20% FOR FRICTION	60	90	135
1970	2DRHT	GTX	JOH	DRIVER'S TRAINING CAR	100	165	200
1971	2DRHT	ROADRUNNER	MPC		90	135	185
1971	2DRHT	ROADRUNNER	MPC	DRIVER'S TRAINING CAR	100	165	215

1961 Plymouth Valiant by SMP

1973 Plymouth Duster by MPC

1966 Plymouth Barracuda by AMT

1970 Plymouth Barracuda by MPC

1951 Pontiac Chieftain Eight by AMT

1959 Pontiac Bonneville by AMT

✦✦ PLASTIC PROMOTIONALS ✦✦

YEAR	STYLE	SERIES	MAKER	NOTES	AVG.	GOOD	OPT.

PLYMOUTH, mid-sized, continued

YEAR	STYLE	SERIES	MAKER	NOTES	AVG.	GOOD	OPT.
1972	2DRHT	ROADRUNNER	MPC		75	115	150
1973	2DRHT	ROADRUNNER	MPC		60	90	125
1974	2DRHT	ROADRUNNER	MPC		30	50	75
1975	2DRHT	ROADRUNNER	MPC		30	40	60

▼▼▼ PLYMOUTH, compact ▼▼▼

YEAR	STYLE	SERIES	MAKER	NOTES	AVG.	GOOD	OPT.
1960	4DR	VALIANT	SMP	+20% FOR TORSION BARS	40	75	100
1961	4DR	VALIANT	SMP		90	125	175
1962	2DRHT	VALIANT	AMT		150	275	400
1963	2DRHT	VALIANT	AMT	-20% FOR FRICTION	40	75	100
1964	2DRHT	VALIANT	AMT	-20% FOR FRICTION	85	135	200
1965	2DRHT	VALIANT	AMT		150	200	325
1966	2DRHT	VALIANT	AMT		185	300	475
1971	2DR	DUSTER	MPC	+100% FOR PLUM CRAZY COLOR	80	115	175
1972	2DR	DUSTER	MPC		70	95	135
1973	2DR	DUSTER	MPC		40	65	100
1974	2DR	DUSTER	MPC		35	50	75
1977	2DR	VOLARE	MPC		-	20	40
1978	2DR	VOLARE	MPC		-	20	40

▼▼▼ PLYMOUTH BARRACUDA ▼▼▼

YEAR	STYLE	SERIES	MAKER	NOTES	AVG.	GOOD	OPT.
1964	2DRHT	BARRACUDA	AMT	FASTBACK,"VALIANT" ON REAR, -30% FOR FRICTION	80	115	185
1965	2DRHT	BARRACUDA	AMT	FASTBACK, -30% FOR FRICTION	80	115	185
1966	2DRHT	BARRACUDA	AMT	FASTBACK, -30% FOR FRICTION	70	100	165
1967	2DRHT	BARRACUDA	AMT	FASTBACK	85	150	225
1968	2DRHT	BARRACUDA	MPC	FASTBACK	85	150	225
1969	2DRHT	BARRACUDA	MPC	FASTBACK	80	125	185
1970	2DRHT	BARRACUDA	MPC	+50% FOR PLUM CRAZY COLOR	200	300	385
1971	2DRHT	BARRACUDA	MPC	+50% FOR PLUM CRAZY COLOR	250	350	435
1972	2DRHT	BARRACUDA	MPC		90	175	275

▼▼▼ PONTIAC, full-sized ▼▼▼

YEAR	STYLE	SERIES	MAKER	NOTES	AVG.	GOOD	OPT.
1951	4DR	CHIEFTAIN SIX	AMT	-10% FOR NO WINDOWS	60	125	150
1951	4DR	CHIEFT. EIGHT	AMT	-10% FOR NO WINDOWS	50	90	125
1952	4DR	CHIEFTAIN	AMT	-10% FOR NO WINDOWS	60	90	150
1953	2DRHT	CHIEFTAIN	AMT	-10% FOR FRICTION & NO WINDOWS	40	80	100
1954	2DRHT	CHIEFTAIN	AMT	-10% FOR FRICTION & NO WINDOWS	40	90	125
1955	4DR	STAR CHIEF	JOH	-10% FOR FRICTION	40	90	125
1955	4DR	STAR CHIEF	IDEAL		40	90	125
1955	2DRHT	STAR CHIEF	JOH	-10% FOR FRICTION, REISSUE EXISTS	40	90	125
1955	2DRHT	STAR CHIEF	IDEAL		40	90	125
1956	4DRHT	STAR CHIEF	JOH	-10% FOR FRICTION, REISSUE EXISTS	40	90	125
1957	4DRHT	STAR CHIEF	SMP	PLATED, +10% FOR NASCAR VICTORY TROPHY	100	175	225
1957	4DRHT	STAR CHIEF	SMP	PLASTIC CHASSIS W/ NO INTERIOR	40	75	100
1957	4DRHT	STAR CHIEF	SMP	METAL CHASSIS W/ NO INTERIOR, -20% FOR INCORRECT HUBCAPS	20	40	60
1957	4DRHT	STAR CHIEF	SMP	METAL CHASSIS W/ INTERIOR., -20% FOR INCORRECT HUBCAPS	40	75	100
1957	CONV.	STAR CHIEF	SMP	PLASTIC CHASSIS, RESIN REISSUE EXISTS	100	185	250
1957	CONV.	STAR CHIEF	SMP	METAL CHASSIS, -20% INCORRECT HUBCAPS	90	125	150
1958	2DRHT	BONNEVILLE	AMT	PLATED	125	175	225
1958	2DRHT	BONNEVILLE	AMT	ALL VERSIONS, -20% FOR GOLD SIDE SPEAR & COVE	60	125	175
1958	CONV.	BONNEVILLE	AMT	-20% FOR GOLD SIDE SPEAR/COVE	80	130	200
1959	2DRHT	BONNEVILLE	AMT	+10% FOR COASTER	40	80	115
1959	2DRHT	BONNEVILLE	AMT	PLATED, +10% FOR KNUDSEN TROPHY	150	175	225
1959	CONV.	BONNEVILLE	AMT	+10% FOR COASTER	50	90	165
1960	2DRHT	BONNEVILLE	AMT	+20% FOR CHASSIS MARKED "WIDE-TRACK"	40	65	110

5-41

1964 Pontiac Bonneville by AMT

1970 Pontiac Bonneville by MPC

1970 Pontiac Grand Prix by MPC

1969 Pontiac Firebird by MPC

1974 Pontiac Firebird 400 by MPC

1968 Pontiac GTO by MPC

✦✦ PLASTIC PROMOTIONALS ✦✦

YEAR	STYLE	SERIES	MAKER	NOTES	AVG.	GOOD	OPT.
PONTIAC, full-sized, continued							
1960	2DRHT	BONNEVILLE	AMT	PLATED	100	175	225
1960	CONV.	BONNEVILLE	AMT	+20% FOR CHASSIS MARKED "WIDE-TRACK"	45	85	135
1961	2DRHT	BONNEVILLE	AMT	+30% FOR PLASTIC CHASSIS	40	75	125
1961	CONV.	BONNEVILLE	AMT	+30% FOR PLASTIC CHASSIS	50	90	150
1962	2DRHT	BONNEVILLE	AMT	-30% FOR FRICTION	115	185	275
1962	CONV.	BONNEVILLE	AMT	-30% FOR FRICTION	150	225	325
1963	2DRHT	BONNEVILLE	AMT	-20% FOR FRICTION	65	115	165
1963	CONV.	BONNEVILLE	AMT	-20% FOR FRICTION	75	135	185
1964	2DRHT	BONNEVILLE	AMT	-20% FOR FRICTION	70	125	175
1964	2DRHT	GRAND PRIX	AMT	-20% FOR FRICTION	70	125	175
1964	CONV.	BONNEVILLE	AMT	-20% FOR FRICTION	75	135	185
1965	2DRHT	BONNEVILLE	AMT		75	135	185
1965	2DRHT	GRAND PRIX	AMT		75	135	185
1965	CONV.	BONNEVILLE	AMT		90	150	225
1966	2DRHT	BONNEVILLE	MPC		75	135	185
1966	CONV.	BONNEVILLE	PMC		90	150	225
1967	2DRHT	BONNEVILLE	MPC		65	115	165
1967	CONV.	BONNEVILLE	MPC		75	125	185
1968	2DRHT	BONNEVILLE	MPC		50	90	135
1968	CONV.	BONNEVILLE	MPC		50	115	165
1969	2DRHT	BONNEVILLE	MPC		40	75	125
1969	2DRHT	GRAND PRIX	MPC		50	85	135
1969	CONV.	BONNEVILLE	MPC		50	85	135
1970	2DRHT	BONNEVILLE	MPC	-20% FOR BANK	40	75	115
1970	2DRHT	GRAND PRIX	MPC		50	85	125
1970	CONV.	BONNEVILLE	MPC		60	95	135
1971	2DRHT	GRAND PRIX	MPC		50	85	125
1972	2DRHT	GRAND PRIX	MPC		50	85	125
▾▾▾ PONTIAC FIREBIRD ▾▾▾							
1967	2DRHT		MPC		90	125	200
1967	CONV.		MPC		100	150	235
1968	2DRHT		MPC		100	175	250
1968	CONV.		MPC		125	200	300
1969	2DRHT		MPC		90	145	225
1969	CONV.		MPC		100	175	250
1970	2DR		MPC		40	65	125
1971	2DR	400	MPC		40	65	125
1972	2DR	400	MPC		40	65	125
1973	2DR	400	MPC		30	50	100
1974	2DR	400	MPC		30	50	100
1975	2DR		MPC	UNBUILT KIT, -30% IF BUILT	-	-	50
1976	2DR		MPC	UNBUILT KIT, -30% IF BUILT	-	-	40
1977	2DR		MPC	UNBUILT KIT, -30% IF BUILT	-	-	30
1978	2DR		MPC	UNBUILT KIT, -30% IF BUILT	-	-	30
1979	2DR		MPC	UNBUILT KIT, -30% IF BUILT	-	-	30
1980	2DR		MPC	UNBUILT KIT, -30% IF BUILT	-	-	30
▾▾▾ PONTIAC GTO ▾▾▾							
1965	2DRHT		AMT		125	250	385
1965	CONV.		AMT		125	250	385
1966	2DRHT		MPC		175	300	435
1966	2DRHT		MPC	TIGER PAW/ THOM McCANN, SIMPLIFIED CHASSIS	185	310	435
1966	CONV.		MPC		175	325	475
1967	2DRHT		MPC		175	300	400
1967	2DRHT		MPC	THOM McCANN	185	310	425
1967	CONV.		MPC		185	325	425
1968	2DRHT		MPC	+30 % FOR MOTOR TREND "CAR OF THE YEAR"	100	175	275
1968	CONV.		MPC		125	200	325

1970 Pontiac GTO by MPC

1962 Pontiac Le Mans by AMT

1964 Pontiac Le Mans by AMT

1957-62 Renault Dauphine by Hubley

1955 Studebaker Commander by AMT

1958-62 Triumph TR3 by Hubley

✦✦ PLASTIC PROMOTIONALS ✦✦

<u>YEAR</u>	<u>STYLE</u>	<u>SERIES</u>	<u>MAKER</u>	<u>NOTES</u>	<u>AVG.</u>	<u>GOOD</u>	<u>OPT.</u>

PONTIAC GTO, continued

YEAR	STYLE	SERIES	MAKER	NOTES	AVG.	GOOD	OPT.
1969	2DRHT		MPC		100	165	235
1969	CONV.		MPC		115	185	300
1970	2DRHT		MPC	RED WITH MICHIGAN PLATE	40	70	100
1970	2DRHT		MPC	WITH 1970 PLATE	50	90	125
1971	2DRHT		MPC		75	115	175
1972	2DRHT		MPC		75	115	175

▾▾▾ PONTIAC, TEMPEST & LE MANS ▾▾▾

YEAR	STYLE	SERIES	MAKER	NOTES	AVG.	GOOD	OPT.
1961	4DR	TEMPEST	AMT	-30% FOR FRICTION	40	75	100
1962	2DRHT	LE MANS	AMT	-30% FOR FRICTION	50	90	125
1962	CONV.	LE MANS	AMT	-30% FOR FRICTION	60	95	135
1963	2DRHT	LE MANS	AMT		75	150	175
1963	CONV.	LE MANS	AMT		90	135	185
1964	2DRHT	LE MANS	AMT		100	175	300
1964	CONV.	LE MANS	AMT		115	185	335

▾▾▾ RENAULT ▾▾▾

YEAR	STYLE	SERIES	MAKER	NOTES	AVG.	GOOD	OPT.
1957-62	4DR	DAUPHINE	HUB	1/24TH, -20% FOR NO WINDOWS & NO INTERIOR	20	40	65

▾▾▾ ROLLS ROYCE ▾▾▾

YEAR	STYLE	SERIES	MAKER	NOTES	AVG.	GOOD	OPT.
1960	4DR	SILVER CLOUD	HUB	1/24TH	25	50	100

▾▾▾ STUDEBAKER ▾▾▾

YEAR	STYLE	SERIES	MAKER	NOTES	AVG.	GOOD	OPT.
1950	2DR	STARLIGHT	AMT	ALL VERSIONS	75	100	200
1951	2DR	STARLIGHT	AMT	ALL VERSIONS	90	125	225
1952	2DR	STARLIGHT	AMT	-30% FOR NO WINDOWS	60	90	150
1953	2DRHT	COMMANDER	AMT	-30% FOR NO WINDOWS	60	90	150
1954	2DRHT	COMMANDER	AMT	-30% FOR NO WINDOWS	60	90	150
1955	2DRHT	COMMANDER	AMT	-30% FOR NO WINDOWS	70	115	165
1956	2DRHT	GOLDEN HAWK	AMT	WITH TWO-COLOR DECK LID	80	150	175
1956	2DRHT	GOLDEN HAWK	AMT	WITH SINGLE-COLOR DECK LID	75	115	150
1959	2DRHT	LARK	JOH	-20% FOR BLACKWALLS	40	60	115
1960	2DRHT	LARK	JOH	-30% FOR NO INTERIOR	50	75	125
1961	2DRHT	LARK	JOH		60	90	135
1962	2DRHT	LARK	JOH	REISSUE EXISTS	20	40	100
1962	CONV.	LARK	JOH	REISSUE EXISTS	20	50	115

▾▾▾ TRAILWAYS BUS ▾▾▾

YEAR	STYLE	SERIES	MAKER	NOTES	AVG.	GOOD	OPT.
1955	BUS		PMC	DELUXE WITH OPENING COMPARTMENTS	150	225	350
1955	BUS		PMC	WARPING PLASTIC, NO OPENING COMPARTMENTS	90	125	225
1955	BUS		PMC	NON-WARPING PLASTIC, NO OPENING COMPARTMENTS	100	150	250

▾▾▾ TRIUMPH ▾▾▾

YEAR	STYLE	SERIES	MAKER	NOTES	AVG.	GOOD	OPT.
1958-62	CONV.	TR3	HUB	WITH HARD TOP, 1/24TH, -50% FOR NO WINDOWS	75	100	175
1958-62	CONV.	TR3	HUB	1/24TH, -50 % FOR NO WINDOWS	75	100	175

▾▾▾ VOLKSWAGEN ▾▾▾

YEAR	STYLE	SERIES	MAKER	NOTES	AVG.	GOOD	OPT.
1959	2DR	1200	PMC	-30% FOR NO WINDOWS OR NO INTERIOR	40	65	100
1959	2DR	KARMAN GHIA	PMC	-30% FOR NO WINDOWS OR NO INTERIOR	45	75	125

The 1949-65 White 3000 semi is among the finest made plastic promotionals. The White was a popular truck, and the van trailer was readily adaptable for private label promotionals as well. The Mason-Dixon version is presented below along with two views of its original box.

<h1 align="center">◆◆ PLASTIC PROMOTIONALS ◆◆</h1>

YEAR	STYLE	SERIES	MAKER	NOTES	AVG.	GOOD	OPT.
▾▾▾ WHITE TRUCKS ▾▾▾							
1949-65	SEMI	3000	TOP	YELLOW TRAILER, +10% FOR PRIVATE LABEL	350	500	850
1949-65	SEMI	3000	TOP	LT. GRAY TRAILER, +10% FOR PRIVATE LABEL	365	575	900
1949-65	SEMI	3000	TOP	1958 NAT'L TRUCK ROADEO MARKINGS	435	675	1200
1949-65	SEMI	3000	TOP	MASON-DIXON MARKINGS	450	685	1250
1949-65	SEMI	3000	TOP	COOP LUBRICANTS MARKINGS	475	700	1275
1949-65	SEMI	3000TD	TOP	DIESEL, +20% FOR PRIVATE LABEL TRAILER	500	750	1375
▾▾▾ WILLYS & JEEP ▾▾▾							
1953	2DR	AERO	BIRD	RESIN REISSUE EXISTS	150	250	350
1953	2DR	AERO	BIRD	. . . .	150	250	350

The White 3000 promotional by Topping was adapted, probably for award purposes, for the 1958
National Truck Roadeo. In this example the trailer is molded in white and the trailer markings
are applied by heat stamp as opposed to decals.

Mr. Dealer: BOOST YOUR SALES WITH Hubley SCALE MODEL
'61 METROPOLITANS

AUTHORIZED & APPROVED BY AMERICAN MOTORS

USE THEM TO PROMOTE YOUR BUSINESS, MAKE MORE SALES.

- DEALER PROMOTION
- TEST-DRIVE INCENTIVE
- AUTO SHOW USE
- DIRECT MAIL PREMIUMS

NO. 1207 METROPOLITAN HARD-TOP—An authentic 1/24th scale model made of cellulose acetate. Full detailed chassis showing frame, muffler, tailpipe, differential, etc. The powerful friction motor gives added play value and appeal. Accessory parts chrome-plated. White wall tires, windshield and windows. Interiors in full detail with dashboard, steering wheel and seats. Individually boxed. Packed 1 dozen per shipping carton.

NO. 158K METROPOLITAN CONVERTIBLE KIT—This beautiful customizing kit includes body, interior, dashboard, steering wheel, detailed chassis, axles, white wall tires and screws plus chrome-plated accessory parts.

Parts for customizing include chrome-plated aerials, tailpipe extensions, spotlights, fender mirrors, fender skirts, spare wheel cover, and many others. Packed 1 dozen per shipping carton.

NO. 1208 METROPOLITAN CONVERTIBLE—Includes all details as listed for Hardtop. Packed 1 dozen per shipping carton.

THE HUBLEY MANUFACTURING CO., LANCASTER, PA., U.S.A.

ORDER BLANK

Send your order today
THE HUBLEY MANUFACTURING CO., LANCASTER, PA., U. S. A.

_____ dozen #1207 @ $16.00 per dozen*   _____ dozen #1208 @ $16.00 per dozen*   _____ dozen #158K @ $12.00 per dozen*

*Minimum order—not broken   All prices include shipping charges.   Please send check with this order.

NAME_______________________________________

STREET_________________________ CITY________________ STATE________

Authorized Signature________________________ Position______________

The Hubley Manufacturing Company of Lancaster, Pennsylvania, an old and well-established toy maker, ventured briefly into the promotional arena. Hubley produced the following vehicles:

> 1960 Ford Fairlane 4dr
> 1960 Ford Country Sedan
> 1961 Ford Fairlane 4dr
> 1961 Ford Country Sedan
> 1962 Ford Country Sedan
> 1958-53 Mercedes-Benz 300SL 2dr
> 1958-53 Mercedes-Benz 300SL convertible
> 1959-62 Metropolitan 2dr
> 1959-62 Metropolitan convertible
> 1957-62 Renault Dauphine 4dr
> 1960 Rolls Royce 4dr
> 1958-62 Triumph TR3 convertible
> 1958-62 Triumph TR3 convertible with hard top

On the opposing page is the order form sent to Nash dealers by Hubley for ordering the 1961 Metropolitan. Although all Metropolitans for that year were two-tone cars, some of the promotionals delivered were solid color vehicles. A Metropolitan ordered using the form is pictured below.

1974 AMC Hornet by Jo-Han

1950 Chevrolet Styleline by Banthrico

1966 AMC Ambassador by Jo-Han

1969 Oldsmobile 4-4-2 by Jo-Han

1949 Chrysler New Yorker by National Products

1952 Ford F-1 panel by National Products

Ford distributed promotionals both at dealerships and through mailings. The vehicles were packaged in boxes of different design and construction. The black 1963 Thunderbird is pictured beside its dealership box. The red 1963 Thunderbird is shown atop its mailer box. That box has a cardboard liner for added rigidity and a blank external panel for addressing and postage.

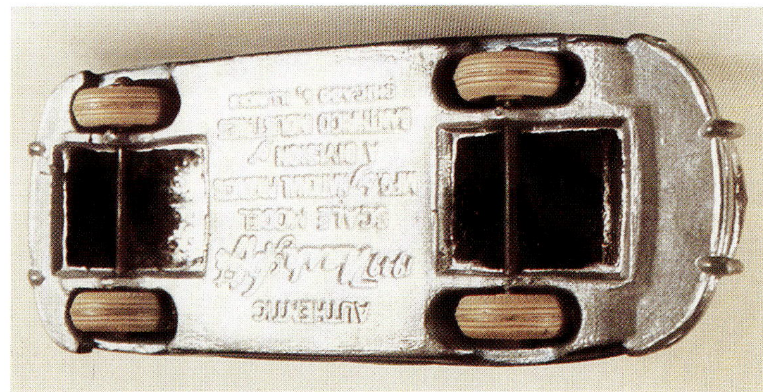

Nash made minimal design changes between the 1949 and 1950 model years. The rear window of the 1949 on the left is smaller and more oval than that on the 1950 on the right. To confuse subsequent collectors, the underside on many of the 1950 Nashes have "1949" in the casting as pictured in the right photo.

1966 Plymouth Fury III by Jo-Han

1940 Buick Super by National Products

1957-63 Willys FC-170 pickup by Authenticast

1971 Chevrolet Camaro SS by MPC

1967 Chevrolet Impala SS by AMT

1968 Plymouth Barracuda by MPC

The 1946-49 Willys Jeep pickups appear in at least two versions. The one on the left is dark burgundy with cream wheel centers and a long hood center trim. The pickup on the right is lighter, more maroon, with yellow wheel centers and a short hood trim.

It would be virtually impossible to improve upon this 1969 Dodge Coronet. In addition to its superior condition, the car comes with its original box, which is color designated to match the car, and with the original decals, which are not applied. The condition of both the box and the decals matches that of the car.

The popularity of the promotional Thunderbirds from the 1950's suffers from the warping plastic used in their production. This condition is evident in the bowing of the windshield frame and sides of the 1956 above. The 1957 model pictured below is not warped as badly and is unusual in the light green color shown. Red 1957 Thunderbirds, however, are extremely common and worth considerably less than other colors.

1965 Ford Falcon by AMT

1953 Dodge Coronet by Banthrico

1966 Chevrolet Impala by AMT

1957 Desoto Fireflite by Jo-Han

1965 Rambler Marlin by Jo-Han

1961 Ford Galaxie by AMT

Some promotionals were used for wide-scale manufacturer giveaway programs. The 1958 Edsel two-door hardtop in turquoise and white is one example. That color and model Edsel was distributed in huge quantities to persons who test drove the full-sized car when it was first introduced for the 1958 model year. The postcard extending this offer to the buying public is presented above. One of these Edsels is pictured below with the original 12-pack shipping carton and several individual boxes. Because this car in this color combination is very common, its value is considerably less than the same vehicle in other colors. (Note that the pictured example has 1958 Ford hubcaps, a typical production error.)

Studebaker did not materially change the design of its model 2R stake truck from 1949 through 1953. Therefore, the same molds could be used for promotionals without change for multiple years. During this same time period, National Products had been acquired and completely merged into Banthrico. The company adopted 1/25th as its standard promotional scale except for situations such as with this smaller scale Studebaker where the design remained unchanged. The red truck above has white Firestone tires mounted on metal hubs. It was probably a 1949 issue, while the green example below atop its original box was likely issued a couple of years later because it has unmarked black rubber tires with no hubs.

1948 Ford St. Louis police car by Master Caster

1971 Pontiac Firebird 400 by MPC

1948-50 Dodge pickup by National Products

1972 Ford Mustang Mach I by AMT

1950 Chevrolet Styleline by Banthrico

1958 Imperial Crown by SMP

Pictured on the opposing page is an opened case of 1954 Chevrolet promotionals as shipped by PMC to the dealerships for the 1954 model year. One of the promotionals, a white over green 150 two-door is pictured separately.   Below is a blue and white 1956 Chevrolet Bel Air two-door hardtop, also still in its original cellophane wrapper. Chevrolet dealership cars were wrapped per these examples from 1951 through 1956, while the retail store versions were individually boxed. Collectors of new/boxed dealership promotionals face a dilemma for these model year Chevrolets.

When writing a book, an author has many choices. Some of the choices in regard to this book on promotionals included the years to cover, color references, number and content of photos, and much more. The first fifty years were selected for coverage for several reasons, but primarily because that time frame includes most promotionals of established interest and with established collectible values. Color references were generally limited to those instances where the color has a definite impact on value. There will be rare instances where a color and/or condition will press the extreme limits of scarcity and warrant a premium value. However, expanding the listings to provide for all colors for each vehicle would result in a book several times as big, more costly and still incomplete. The photos presented are in general proportion to the number of promotionals issued by make. This was deemed the best approach although some collectors would prefer more Mopar photos and others, perhaps, more Chevrolet, etc.

Thus, the above and other choices were made. As a result you are now holding a book that lists 1,082 promotional vehicles. That's quite a large number and certainly beyond most people's memory capacity, especially when three values are provided for each. The book also contains 250 photos, all in color, which represent a good cross section of the promotional vehicles that were produced. These listings and photos are intended to add to your enjoyment in collecting promotionals. That's what it's all about, enjoyment. So, have a good time!